How to Crack
Cryptic
Crosswords

How to Crack

Cryptic

Crosswords

Hints and Tricks to help you find the answers

VIVIEN HAMPSHIRE

howtobooks

Constable & Robinson Ltd
55–56 Russell Square
London WC1B 4HP
www.constablerobinson.com

First published in the UK by How To Books,
an imprint of Constable & Robinson Ltd, 2013

A copy of the British Library Cataloguing in
Publication Data is available from the British Library

ISBN 978-1-84528-508-1

Printed and bound in the UK

1 3 5 7 9 10 8 6 4 2

This book is dedicated to my dad, Wilfred Smith,
who taught me the art of the cryptic crossword and
without whom I really wouldn't have had a clue!

Contents

1 Introduction

Are you baffled by cryptic crosswords? Do you want to increase your word power and exercise your brain, but can't make any sense of the clues? There is no secret formula to cracking the cryptic crossword. Anyone can do it. This book is packed with all the know-how, hints and tricks you will ever need to help you find the right answers every time. From clever to cunning to downright devious, all the different types of clue are here, with tips on how to recognise them, interpret them and, of course, solve them!

Cryptic crosswords appear regularly in newspapers and magazines, many of them offering the chance of a prize – usually either cash, books or a posh pen. Find out what makes these puzzles so intriguing, yet so infuriating. With around 150 clues analysed and explained in full, you will soon be on your way to the satisfaction of completing your first crossword grid, impressing your family, friends and fellow commuters, and maybe even winning a prize!

A LITTLE BIT OF HISTORY

Crosswords are reputed to be the most popular word game in the world, but as a pastime for adults they have only been around for about a hundred years. Although

1

they had existed in some form or another in England since the 19th century, they were then mainly simple word squares designed to amuse children, grouping letters together in such a way that the same words could be read both vertically and horizontally.

The first known published example of a crossword intended for adults was laid out in a diamond shape, with interlocking words but no black squares, and contained simple non-cryptic clues. It appeared in a New York newspaper in 1913, although its creator, Arthur Wynne, was a Liverpool man.

During the following decade, the new crossword puzzle craze swept America, the now familiar black and white squares format was born, and puzzles became a regular feature in almost every newspaper. In 1922, they made the leap across the Atlantic and arrived in the UK, where more difficult cryptic versions soon began to develop. The now famous *Times* crossword made its debut in 1930.

DISCOVERING CROSSWORDS

So, what makes crossword puzzles so popular? Who is spending so much time and effort worrying over them and filling them in, and why?

The Benefits

There is something very satisfying about completing a crossword puzzle. Crosswords present a challenge. They make you think. They help you to keep your brain function in good working order and slow down the memory loss that inevitably creeps up on us as we get older. In fact, solving a daily puzzle has been shown to help reduce the risk of dementia and Alzheimer's, or at least to delay its onset.

From the simplest clues you might find in a magazine's 'coffee break' puzzle page to the real stinkers in the more high-brow daily newspapers (the sort of clues that can take hours to understand, let alone solve!) there is a definite sense of achievement when you see those little white boxes in the grid slowly filling up as you get nearer and nearer to completing your puzzle.

It's a fascinating hobby that costs very little to pursue. Unless you are taking the whole thing very seriously indeed and travelling the world to compete in crossword competitions (and, yes, some people do!) it's usually just the cost of a magazine, newspaper or puzzle book, and the pen or pencil needed to write in the answers!

Filling in a crossword helps to pass the time on boring train journeys, and gives you something relaxing to do while you drink your morning coffee, laze in a hot bath or have your hair done. But 'doing' a crossword offers much more than just an hour or two of idle fun. It can also help us to improve our spelling and vocabulary, expand our general knowledge and, if we manage to finish it, boost our self-esteem. A bit like playing a game of Scrabble® or Boggle®, it lets us explore language, learn new words, and play around with letters in a fun way – but without the need for a board, a timer or an opponent. Crosswords are usually a much more solitary pursuit, which makes their successful completion all the more satisfying. And we all like to feel intelligent, and proud of ourselves, from time to time!

But, of course, crosswords can be infuriating too. There have been many times when I've sat for hours, pen in hand, unable to concentrate on anything else, determined to finish a devilishly difficult puzzle, no matter how long it takes. And nights when I've been unable to go to bed knowing that there is still one unsolved clue staring up at me. There have even been a few occasions when I've been forced to admit defeat and had to wait a day or two for the answers to be published in a later edition of the newspaper before achieving anything like peace of mind. That's how addictive crosswords can become.

Starting Young

I grew up with crosswords. In fact, I can't remember a time when they were not an important part of my daily life. Solving them was something my dad taught me to do when I was very young, and became an enjoyable task that we always undertook together.

As a child, pulling the big dictionaries and atlases of the world from their place on the bookshelf and laying them out on the carpet to help me find the answers – and how to spell them – was always a thrill. Somehow, despite the amazingly extensive content and speed of the internet (which can be a great help to puzzlers now, but had not yet been invented when I started out), I still feel there's

4

nothing quite like poring over a pile of dusty old reference books to track down the information you need.

I'm sure that discovering crosswords at a young age also went a long way towards helping me to develop some of the important skills that have stood me in good stead in later life: how to concentrate, be patient, persistent, self-confident and determined, and – if something matters enough – not to give up. I learned how to relish silence and be content in my own company, and I acquired a curiosity about, and a real love for, words – an ideal grounding for someone who went on to make her living as a writer.

But, as an intelligent and enquiring child, the simple general knowledge puzzles were never going to be able to enthral me for long. The clues, and their answers, were just too uncomplicated and straightforward. Even when my home reference book collection was no match for a particularly tricky question, and a visit to the public library was needed, there was still no real magic in being able to solve them. After all, anyone can find the answers to factual questions if they make the effort and look in the right places.

So, I needed something more. By the age of ten, I had discovered the joys of cryptic crosswords, with their much cleverer and more thought-provoking clues and, under my dad's guidance, was starting to learn how to crack them. And from that moment on, I never looked back!

Who Does Crosswords?

Crosswords know no barriers. Men, women and children all over the world take up the challenge every day. And the rich and famous are just as likely to be crossword addicts as you or I.

When Patrick Creadon, an American film-maker, made a documentary film called *Wordplay* in 2006, which took a look at the highly competitive and rather obsessive world of crossword competitions, he even persuaded ex-President Bill Clinton to talk about his love of solving crosswords and to be filmed working on one.

When TV personality Stephen Fry spent some time in prison as a young man, it is reported that his mother would take him bundles of crosswords cut from copies of *The Times* to keep him busy in his cell. He has also talked publicly about his childhood memories of his parents regularly completing *The Times* crossword together as a team, his mother solving some of the clues and his father coming up with answers for the rest. It was only, he said, because he had inherited the best bits from each of them, that he was able to tackle and finish the puzzles all by himself.

Perhaps the most famous fictional crossword fan was Inspector Morse, created by author Colin Dexter, himself a dedicated crossword buff. The late John Thaw, the actor who played Morse in the TV series, was once quoted as saying that in the same way that Morse is fascinated by crosswords, it is the puzzle of the murder that drives him on. Perhaps many of us just naturally enjoy having something to work out, or a mystery we feel compelled to try to solve. For those of us without a murder to work on, crosswords are certainly able to provide us with the next best thing!

On a more light-hearted note, the comedian Tommy Cooper was always known for his terribly corny, but still very funny, jokes. One of them went like this:

> *A friend of mine rang and asked me to help him with the crossword. The clue was 'a flightless bird found in Iceland', and the answer was two words, six and seven letters long.*
>
> *'I've got it,' I said... 'Frozen chicken!'*

A bird can't be much more flightless – or lifeless – than that! But, of course, if you only know Iceland as a country and have never heard of the frozen food retailer, then the joke, and the clue, will mean nothing to you. Quite often, as we shall see when we start to look more closely at the structure and wording of crossword clues later in this book, even solving a cryptic clue still requires an element of general or more specialised knowledge if it is to make any sense at all.

WHAT DOES CRYPTIC MEAN?

I have talked about moving on from solving straightforward general knowledge clues to tackling the more complex cryptic crossword. But, what exactly do we mean by cryptic?

Any dictionary will tell you that the definition of the word *cryptic* is 'mysterious or obscure in meaning', and that's not a bad explanation of what a cryptic crossword is. Some dictionaries will then go on to tell you that, as far as crosswords are concerned, cryptic clues are difficult clues which indicate their solutions *indirectly.*

And, yes, it's true. A typical cryptic clue does tend to go about things in a complicated, indirect, and some might say devious, way. We are no longer simply looking for the capital city of Poland, who wrote *Aida,* or another word for mother-of-pearl. Now we are starting to mix letters up in anagrams, read words from back to front, pick out alternate or initial letters, search for hidden words and double meanings, and all manner of other similar wordplay tricks. And all without any sort of map to show us which way to go!

The answers won't be easy to find just by opening up a dictionary or an encyclopaedia. With most cryptic clues, not even the wonders of the internet will be able to help you, unless it's to access one of the many 'answer-bank' sites that now give frustrated crossword puzzlers the chance to share their unsolved clues and compare possible answers with each other. I call that cheating, but I will tell you more about where to find that kind of help in Chapter 2.

No, the only way to tackle a cryptic crossword without outside assistance is by thinking things through. Brainpower is needed – and it's a special kind of brainpower that, even if you don't think you have it yet, you can certainly learn to acquire. Cryptic clues deliberately set out to mislead you, making you follow anything but the obvious path to get to the answer. In fact, the more obscure the clues, and the harder they are to solve, the happier the most committed and passionate crossword fan will be. It's their very complexity that makes these particular puzzles so challenging and so compelling.

Songwriter Stephen Sondheim once said that the nice thing about doing a crossword puzzle is that you know there is a solution. For many of us, that's a very comforting thought. No matter how hard the puzzle may seem to be, there is always an answer and, in this book, I am going to show you how to work out what it is.

2 Let's Get Started

First let's look at the structure of crosswords and some of the tools you are going to need to help you complete them, before going on to decide which are the right puzzles for you.

WHAT DO CROSSWORDS LOOK LIKE?

The Layout of the Grid

All crosswords have two things in common:

1. Clues leading to words or phrases which have to be written into a series of white spaces going in straight lines either across or down the grid.

2. The way that these white squares (and the black ones that separate them) are laid out on the page.

No matter how large or small, a properly presented puzzle grid is always symmetrical, with the pattern of black and white squares repeated in mirror-image form in opposite corners or, in the most tightly constructed and truly symmetrical puzzles, repeated in all four corners. If, for example, you have five white squares, representing a five-letter answer, starting in the top left corner and going across the puzzle, followed by two black squares, you will also find exactly the same sequence coming back at you towards the centre of the puzzle from the bottom right, or even from all of the other three corners. Does this make a puzzle any easier to solve? Certainly not, but it does give the grid a pleasing appearance and a feeling of completeness that would not exist if the black and white patterns were just randomly created.

Clues are presented beneath the puzzle grid and are listed in two columns – 'Across', representing those answers that will be written across the grid, and 'Down', for those that are written downwards. Each clue is numbered, the number indicating the place in the grid where the first letter of the answer is to be written.

Only the white spaces where an answer word begins are numbered, with the numbers starting in the top left and being allocated sequentially in a left-to-right and then top-to-bottom fashion. Words will frequently cross each other and interlock, so two clues may have to share a number. You may, for example, have two clues where the answers begin in the white square marked as number 1. These clues will then be called 1 across and 1 down.

Once a correct answer has been entered into the grid, some of its letters are likely to fall into the empty spaces belonging to other words that interlock with it in the grid, so the positioning of these letters should then help you to find the answers to some of the remaining unsolved clues.

How Many Letters?

In brackets after each clue we are told how many letters there are in the answer. You might think that this is fairly obvious, as just taking a look at the crossword grid will reveal how many letters are required, but some answers may be hyphenated words (the clue for 'old-fashioned' would, for example, be followed by the numbers 3-9) or could be phrases made up of more than one word (a clue leading to the answer 'a bird in the hand' would be followed, for example, by 1,4,2,3,4), so these bracketed numbers can actually be very useful.

Note also that crossword grids have no room for punctuation, so any hyphens, spaces between words, apostrophes or commas that may be indicated in the clue will not actually appear in the answer.

A long answer, running to more than one word, may have too many letters in it to be able to run across or down the grid in one fell swoop, and may have to be broken up and fitted into two or more different areas of the grid. Taking the example above, 'a bird' might fit into the spaces allocated to 10 across, and the rest of the phrase 'in the hand' might be slotted in at 3 down. Hence 10 across will say 'and 3 down' before giving the wording of the clue, while 3 down will then simply say 'See 10 across'.

Two Sets of Clues

Some crosswords offer one grid but with two sets of different clues – a set of straightforward general knowledge ones, often billed as a 'quick' or 'coffee break' puzzle, and a more complex cryptic set. In some of these puzzles, you have to choose either one set or the other because, although the answers will fit into the same grid pattern, they are not interchangeable. In others, the two sets of clues will lead you to identical answers, so you get to pick and choose. If the cryptic clue is baffling you, try reading the simpler clue as it will get you to the same answer by an easier route! Just make sure which sort of 'two-clues' puzzle you are tackling before you start, as mixing and matching doesn't always work.

WHAT YOU NEED TO GET STARTED

Tools of the Trade

Apart from a few quiet moments and a comfy chair, all you really need to get you started is a crossword suited to your level of ability and a pen or pencil, although there will be times when you realise you have filled in a wrong answer, so some correction fluid or a rubber can be useful extras! If you are hoping to try for some prizes, keep a good supply of envelopes and stamps too, and remember to post in time. Newspapers often print the answers to their daily puzzles only a couple of days later, so entries need to arrive, or at least be postmarked, before the answers have been published.

Books to Help You

Some cryptic clues do still rely on a certain degree of general knowledge, so it helps to keep a good dictionary on standby. This will also come in handy if you need help with how to spell an answer or to double-check a word's meaning. An electronic crossword solver makes a more expensive but very useful alternative. It's easily portable, so can be carried in a handbag or pocket, or in your holiday luggage, and, if you are really stuck but already know a few of the letters in an answer, it can also list all the possible words that fit, and the more sophisticated and expensive ones can also offer you useful dictionary definitions for many of them. A bit of a cheat, but sometimes it's the only way to crack a really difficult clue that is stumping you, and a way to get the puzzle moving again.

Specialist 'crossword key' books work in a similar way, listing all the possible words that will fit once you have the word length and a few letters to start you off, but without giving the meaning of the words as a conventional dictionary does. Other 'crossword companions' or 'crossword dictionaries' may provide lists of words organised firstly into categories (plants, rivers, transport, composers, etc.) and then by the number of letters in each word. These are most useful for helping to solve general knowledge crosswords, offering assistance only for the occasional cryptic clue that might require some specialist knowledge.

Finding Specialist Help

If all else fails, there are always people, and websites, willing to help you. Finding a crossword 'buddy' – a friend or travelling companion who enjoys puzzles as much as you do and reads the same newspaper – will be helpful, as you can discuss particularly troublesome clues, compare answers, or even set up a little healthy competition between you. There's nothing like trying to complete your puzzle more quickly than someone else to spur you on to the end!

The internet is awash with sites where puzzlers can ask for help with, or post their suggested answers to, the crossword clues and quiz questions they are working on. Take a look at *www.theanswerbank.co.uk* or *www.crosswordsolver.org* where finding what you need when you are stuck is usually just a click or two away – and free. Strangely, it is often the general knowledge clues (whose answers should be easy enough to find using an internet search engine) that lazy puzzlers seem to seek the most help with. I do find it amazing that so many people are prepared to freely give away the crossword answers they have slaved over, even to others who may be competing for the same prize.

Last of all, and not something I would ever recommend, is to ring one of the phone numbers some newspapers publish alongside their crosswords. All you will be told is the full solution to the puzzle. You can't usually ask for help with just one clue, and they will not explain how to interpret clues or how answers have been arrived at. These lines generally cost at least 75 pence per minute, and all they are doing is saving you the wait, as the solution is almost always printed in the paper within the next edition or two. Other text message services offered in the press allow you to send in the letters you have already worked out, together with a series of question marks to indicate your missing letters, and they will reply with all the possible words that fit. Again, there will be no explanations or meanings given, nothing offered that a good crossword key book or electronic solver can't provide, and the service comes at a high price.

CHOOSING A PUZZLE

So, that's the basics out of the way – the general layout, rules, tools and help available to you, no matter what type of crossword you are trying to solve. But from now on, this book will be concentrating purely on cryptic crosswords.

Before urging you to pick up your first cryptic crossword and (with the help of this book) try to solve it, it's worth mentioning that there is a world of difference between the level of difficulty of a typical *Times* Crossword clue and one you might find in *The Sun*. I recommend that you start at the easier end, practise as often as you can (preferably daily), take your time to learn the craft, and gradually work your way up.

You will find cryptic crosswords suited to all ability levels in a whole range of local newspapers, women's magazines, church newsletters, puzzle books, etc., and it would be impossible for me to attempt to track them all down and analyse them. But we all have access to the national press, so here is just a quick rundown of the cryptic crosswords currently available in the most popular UK daily and Sunday papers, an idea of how difficult they are, plus some of the possible prizes on offer should you be lucky enough to win.

Crosswords in the National Press

The following listing is in order of difficulty, starting with the easiest. I have given each crossword a star rating for difficulty (up to a maximum of 5 stars), based purely on my own experience and opinion, having studied and completed several example puzzles from each paper. Where a second set of easier clues is provided, I have tried to ignore them for rating purposes and have judged each crossword on its cryptic clues only. Solving these will certainly become easier if you take advantage of the alternative clues, but try to use them as back-up only, for those times when you are genuinely stuck. Information was correct at the time of writing but is subject to change.

■ **The Daily Mirror** offers a daily 'Two Speed Coffee break' crossword with both cryptic and quick clues leading to the same answers. This is a very small grid, just 11 spaces square, which rarely includes an answer longer than 7 letters long. It uses plenty of familiar words that are unlikely to have you reaching for the dictionary. Clues tend to be simple – mainly anagrams, double meanings and answers hidden in the clue itself. Unchallenging, but perfect for the absolute beginner. There is no prize. Answers appear the following day. Difficulty rating *

■ **The Daily Star** offers the 'Two Way Teaser', another small (13 spaces square) and simple crossword, with short single-word answers and a good mix of clue types, some of which are quite poorly written but nevertheless easy to solve. There is a separate set of quick clues running alongside the cryptic ones, which should help if you get stuck, and a costly phone number to call if you can't wait for the solution to appear the next day. There is no prize, so this one is just for fun, and ideal for beginners. A crossword of exactly the same standard and format also appears in **The Daily Star on Sunday**. Difficulty rating **

■ **The Daily Express** carries the 'Crusader', a larger cryptic crossword, 15 spaces square, but with no second set of clues to help you. There is a good mix of clue types, with no nasty tricks. Mainly one-word answers, but there are a few longer phrases included, some of which are split into more than one area of the grid. The Crusader appears in the Saturday edition too. There is one daily prize of £100 cash for the first correct solution sent in by post. Answers are published a few days later, and winners' names after about two weeks. A nice puzzle for the beginner eager to take a small step up and try for a prize. Difficulty rating **

■ **The Sun.** The daily 'Two-Speed Crossword' is another that offers two sets of clues, so the 'coffee time clues' will always help you out if the cryptic ones prove too hard. The grid is 13 x 13, with extra large spaces to fill in, which may help if your handwriting is large or your eyesight poor! Clues are fairly straightforward and not too devious, with plenty of anagrams and simple word play. There are no nasty surprises, and the vocabulary used in both the clues and the answers is generally familiar. The

crossword also appears in Saturday editions and in
The Sun on Sunday, in the same format but without
the extra large squares. There is no prize. Answers
can be checked using a costly phone line, but are
published the next day. Difficulty rating **

■ **The i paper (or i)**, the smaller 'daily briefing' version
of the Independent, offers two cryptic crosswords,
the first being the smallest I have seen anywhere,
with a 6 x 6 square grid and only five clues! This
tiny 'five-clue' crossword is perfect for beginners or
for those times when you only have a minute or two
to spare. Symbols alongside the solutions (which are
published in the same issue) explain which are
anagrams, reversed words etc. Difficulty rating **

■ **The Sunday Express** 'Crusader' is billed as a 'Sunday
joust', involving the crusader knight and his squire.
The puzzle is similar in appearance and size to the
Daily Express version but with the added benefit of
'The Squire's clues' – a second set of quick general
knowledge clues that lead to the same answers. There
is one £100 cash prize on offer. Despite the second
set of clues, I found this crossword a little harder
than the daily one, with some clues perhaps a little
obscure. The solutions appear the following Sunday.
Difficulty rating ***

■ **The Daily Mail** cryptic crossword is a standard-sized
grid (15 spaces square), which appears Monday to
Friday, with just one set of clues, combining a wide
and thought-provoking range of clue types. There are

some longer phrases included in the answers, and others may rely on a little general knowledge. There are three daily prizes of £20 each, with completed puzzles to be postmarked no later than the next day. A challenging and satisfying puzzle, with clues that don't leave you feeling baffled or cheated, and ideal for those moving up to intermediate level. Solutions appear in the paper three days after each crossword is published, with lists of recent winners' names on Mondays. Difficulty rating ***

■ **The Daily Mail (Saturday edition)** includes 'The Giant Crossword', one of the largest cryptic crosswords around, with a grid of 25 spaces square. There is also a set of quick clues leading to the same answers. Clues are of a similar standard to those in the daily edition, but sadly (considering the extra time and effort needed to complete such a large puzzle) there is no prize. The solution is published the following Monday. Difficulty rating: ***

■ **The Mail on Sunday** has a puzzle pull-out in the middle of its Review supplement. That's where you will find the 'Sir Lancelot and his Page' cryptic crossword, another 15 x 15 square grid with two sets of clues, billed on very similar lines to the Sunday Express's Crusader and Squire as an 'amiable joust', although the clues here are a little less obscure and generally more satisfying to solve. Sadly, the expensive Parker fountain pen prize was withdrawn during 2012, so this puzzle is now just for fun. The solution appears the following weekend. Difficulty rating ***

■ **The Independent** cryptic crossword offers no prizes. It's another standard 15 x 15 grid, by a named compiler, with a mixture of clue types, intelligently written in the main, but with the odd complicated clue that baffles longer than it should! This one offers another infuriating phone line which I hope you will resist in favour of sticking at it the old-fashioned way. You can also view and tackle the daily crossword on their website, where various 'cheat' facilities can be used to reveal specific letters or the answer to any individual clue you may need help with. Difficulty rating ***

■ **The Daily Telegraph,** like the i paper, unusually offers two cryptic crosswords in the same newspaper. The first can be found on the back page, and is a 15 x 15 square grid with a good mix of intelligently composed clues, very similar in standard and tone to the *Daily Mail*'s. No prize is offered. Answers are published the next day. Again, we are given a phone line to call if we just can't wait for help to solve the clues! Difficulty rating ***

■ **The Sunday Telegraph** offers a fountain pen and crossword companion notebook as a weekly prize for solving its cryptic crossword, to be found in the 'Life' supplement's puzzle pages. Another standard 15 x 15 grid, the clues for this one are intelligently written, with a lot of double meanings and words spliced together or cut short to make new ones. There is a refreshing non-reliance on too many anagrams and answers hidden within the clue, so

often favoured by other papers. Solutions are
published two weeks later. Difficulty rating ***

■ **The Observer** gives us the 'Everyman' crossword, to
be found in its 'New Review' supplement. This is a
good mid-range 15 x 15 square grid, not too taxing,
and with a nice mix of clue types, generally cleverly
and intelligently written. The compiler is not afraid
to include some very welcome longer words and
phrases that stretch almost right across the grid.
There are several small book token and dictionary
prizes on offer each Sunday. Solutions are published
two weeks later. Difficulty rating ***

■ **The London Evening Standard** is not available
nationwide, but given free to passengers travelling
on the London Underground, so many of you may
come across it from time to time when travelling in
the capital. The 'Double Crossword' is a small 13 x
13 grid, offering two sets of clues: the 'easy' general
knowledge ones which should present no problems
to the traveller in a hurry, or the cryptic set that
will definitely take a little longer, being a mix of a
few tricky (by which I mean strange and not
particularly well written) clues mixed up among the
generally quite basic ones. Unusually, the two sets
share a grid but are not interchangeable, so you
have to stick to solving one crossword or the other.
Please try to resist using the phone line solution
checker and the mobile phone text message help-
finder which will each cost you more than £1 a
time! Difficulty rating ***

■ **The i paper**'s second cryptic crossword is a 15 x 15 grid, with a good mix of moderate and more challenging clues, and the occasional use of some refreshingly unfamiliar words (like 'hendiadys' or 'imprimatur') which should have you reaching for the dictionary! Perhaps marginally more difficult than the crossword in its sister paper The Independent, although often compiled by the same people. This one has no prizes, except on Saturday where a non-cash prize is offered to one randomly chosen winner. In the issue I studied it was a portable DAB radio, but this may be subject to change. Difficulty rating ****

■ **The Independent on Sunday** offers a 15 x 15 grid with a mix of intelligently written clues, including one or two really tricky ones. There is a range of reference book and dictionary prizes for a winner and five runners-up each week. Difficulty rating ****

■ **The Financial Times** daily cryptic crossword is another 15 x 15 grid, by one of a regular stable of named compilers, offering some clever and challenging clues. The current crossword and around three weeks' previously published puzzles are also available on their website in PDF format, so they can be printed off but not actually filled-in online. Book prizes are available for the Monday and Saturday puzzles only. Solutions appear the next day, or two weeks later when a prize is on offer. Difficulty rating ****

■ **The Times** crossword has a certain reputation for being tricky. It has long been associated with businessmen and commuters, and it is implied that being able to solve it is a real achievement, if not a minor miracle! In fact, it is not that difficult for a reasonably experienced puzzler to crack, and comes nowhere near the *Sunday Times* version or the *Telegraph*'s Toughie for the complexity of its clues. It's another 15 x 15 grid, which disappointingly offers no prize. Presumably the satisfaction of finishing it is enough, although there is a phone helpline if you can't wait for the solution to be published the next day. Difficulty rating ****

■ **The Guardian** cryptic crossword's 15 x 15 grid is another tricky one, equally as tough as *The Times*, mixing up lots of clue types, and needing a high level of expertise and some quite detailed general knowledge to solve. Luckily, there is a potential reward, as the first five correct entries drawn each win book prizes. Entries may be posted or faxed. One of the few puzzles to name its compiler every day. Difficulty rating ****

■ **The Sunday Times** crossword is also 15 spaces square, and names its compiler – deservedly, as credit should be given where it is due, and some of the clues are very clever and devious indeed. Some also require a degree of specialist general knowledge, particularly of composers, writers, etc. Occasionally a clue proves to be a real stinker that will take a lot of cogitating before finally being solved. There is a first prize of a very expensive silver fountain pen to the weekly winner, with ball pens to the three runners-up. Solutions appear the next Sunday. As an added bonus, the paper runs a weekly clue-writing competition, giving you the chance to write your own original cryptic clue for a given word, for a £20 cash prize. Difficulty rating *****

■ **The Daily Telegraph**'s second offering is found on the puzzles page and is called 'The Toughie'. It certainly lives up to its name! This is again a 15 x 15 grid, with no prizes on offer, but the clues here are really devious and cleverly contrived, often involving the need to identify and decipher a combination of several clue 'types' to solve just one answer. You could almost be excused for calling the phone helpline for this one, if only to stop you staring at a blank grid for too long, and to get you started with the first answer or two. An expert puzzle strictly for the experienced, and the hardest I have found in any national newspaper. Solutions are published the next day. Difficulty rating *****

■ **The Sunday Mirror** and **The People** newspapers have puzzle pages, but do not currently include a cryptic crossword.

Types of Clue to Suit You

So, now we are going to move on to looking at the different types of clue you are likely to encounter, no matter how easy or difficult the crossword you choose.

Anagrams, double meanings, words written in reverse, and many more...

All clues (and I really do mean ALL) will fall into one, or in some cases a combination of more than one, of the category types I am going to explain in the following chapters.

We will look at each type in detail, with plenty of examples, all followed by my simple step-by-step guide to how to solve them. You will then get the opportunity, at regular intervals throughout the book, to start solving clues by yourself.

Welcome to your new hobby, and good luck!

3 Tackling Anagrams

I'm not sure why, but when most of us think of cryptic crosswords, the first type of clue that comes to mind is usually the anagram. It's what simple word puzzles are all about.

WHAT IS AN ANAGRAM?

Anagrams are usually one of the most straightforward clues to crack as all the letters we need are there in the clue – and all we have to do is find them, jumble them up and re-arrange them into a new word. It sounds easy but, even with this type of clue, there may be a few extra complications thrown in your way to fool you, as we shall see later in this chapter.

Recognising the Signs

Unfortunately, although many of the simpler more general puzzles may include the abbreviation 'anag' in brackets after a clue to guide you, no well-written cryptic crossword will ever be so forthcoming. In fact, they do not tell us what type of clue we are dealing with at all. We have to work that out for ourselves.

So, how do you recognise anagrams and, more importantly, go about solving them? Let's begin with a simple example. Here's a cryptic clue:

Catch parts after mix-up? (5)

There are two clear pointers here to help us work out what to do:

1. The words 'after mix-up' immediately alert us to the possibility that we are expected to mix up the letters of one or more of the words in the clue to find our answer, therefore this is to be an anagram.

2. We are told the solution has 5 letters. There are only two words in the clue that have five letters in them – 'catch' and 'parts'. So, we have to work out our anagram using the letters from one of those two words. But which one? In this case, as soon as you try to jumble up the five letters of 'catch' you will see that there are no possible combinations that can form a new and valid word.

So, the anagram has to be of PARTS, and the order of wording in the clue points this way too ('parts after mix-up'). There are several ways you can mix these five letters up to form other words. In just a few seconds, I came up with STRAP, TRAPS, SPRAT and PRATS, although that last one could be regarded as a bit dubious as it's obviously slang – but it would normally be acceptable as it is in the dictionary!

But which one of the four possible anagrams is our answer? Look again at the clue. We know why the phrase 'after mix-up' is there (to alert us to the need to find an anagram), and we also know why the word 'parts' is there (that is the word we have to jumble up). The only other section of the clue left unaccounted for is the word 'catch' – so this must be the bit that tells us more about the meaning of the answer we are seeking.

We now know that we have to mix up the five letters of the word 'PARTS' and come up with an answer that in some way means 'catch'. Of course, being a cryptic clue, designed to deliberately mislead us as much as possible, we are not necessarily looking for something that means 'catch' in the sense of catching a ball or even catching a cold. What other sorts of catch are there? Think of fishing, as in 'catch of the day', and look again at the possible anagrams of 'parts'. There can only be one answer that fits the bill.

Solution: SPRAT

So, this clue consisted of three vital parts, all as important as each other. As we examine some more examples, we will see that to be true of all anagram-type clues. There will always be:

1. a word or phrase that lets us know that an anagram is required;

2. a word or phrase consisting of the letters we are to play around with and jumble up;

3. a word or phrase that leads us towards the meaning of the answer.

Some Examples Explained

Here's another cryptic clue:

New owners don't get better (6)

Here, the simple word 'new' is hinting that we are to make a new word (i.e. that this is to be an anagram). As it has six letters, the word we are to mix up is likely to be 'owners'. Of course, 'better' also has six letters, but the order of the wording in this clue makes this an unlikely candidate. It is the word 'owners' that we are being told has to be 'new', so it is those six letters we will work with. The resultant new word, and therefore the answer we are looking for, will mean 'don't get better'.

Solution: WORSEN

The following three clues are fairly simple and straightforward anagrams requiring the mixing up of the letters from one or two words. They all follow the basic rules, as discussed above, and should need no further explanation. Note how each one uses a different pointer word to alert us to the need for an anagram. And they all give a very clear indication, either at the beginning or end of the clue, as to the meaning of the answer.

Taking a nap? Disturb please! (6)

Solution: ASLEEP

Main pit reconstructed for section of orchestra (7)

Solution: TIMPANI

Train up revolutionary Protestant (7)

Solution: PURITAN

Here's a slightly more devious clue:

Nice place in which I arrive shattered (7)

Our pointer word this time is 'shattered'. This implies breaking up, and hence, once we start to get the hang of what possible hints to look out for, leads us to the conclusion that some of the letters are to be broken up, and that this is therefore almost certainly another anagram clue. Now we need to find the seven letters that are to be 'shattered' – but there is no seven letter word in the clue. So, it must be a phrase, or a combination of two or more adjacent words, that we are looking for this time.

Let's try 'I arrive' as that seems to be the part of the clue we are being told gets shattered, and it also contains the magic seven letters.

Now the only section of the clue left that might explain the meaning of the required answer is 'Nice place'. What kind of nice place can we make from the seven letters of 'I arrive'? Write the letters out on a scrap of paper. Try shuffling them into different combinations. When you arrive at the only possible answer, the cleverness of the clue becomes apparent. It didn't mean 'nice' at all, but Nice with a capital N, as in France. Sneaky!

Solution: RIVIERA

And here is another very similar clue, using a different anagram pointer word but leading to exactly the same answer:

Nice here but I arrive in a storm (7)

Solution: RIVIERA

The next one is a much more complex example, borrowed from a crossword in The Observer:

**Need MOT? GT somehow not right,
please understand (4,3,2,5)**

Our answer will require fourteen letters in all, and consists of a four-word phrase.

That little word 'somehow' is clearly the one that points us towards this being an anagram, and it is the letters of the words 'Need MOT? GT' that appear immediately before it which are likely to be the ones we need to mix up. Remember that the punctuation is there to make some sense of the clue but will never appear in the answer, so you can safely ignore the question mark.

But that phrase 'Need MOT? GT' doesn't actually have fourteen letters in it. There are only nine. So, what help can the following words 'not right' give us? When something is not right, it must be wrong. So here we have an anagram that will hopefully lead us to the first nine letters (or in this case, the first three words) of the answer, to be followed by the word 'wrong'. This is the first example we have looked at so far of a clue in two parts, needing two different techniques to be able to solve the whole. In other words, this one is a little more than just an ordinary anagram. There will be plenty more of these 'combined type' clues later in the book.

Now, somewhere in the clue, we should find a hint as to the meaning of the eventual answer, and here it must be the only remaining part of the clue we haven't had to make use of yet: 'please understand.'

Mix up the letters, add the word 'wrong', think of a phrase meaning 'please understand' and we finally come to our answer, which incidentally provides another example of how we must drop the punctuation, because there will be no room in the squares on the crossword grid for the apostrophe.

Solution: DON'T GET ME WRONG

Adding Extra Letters and Taking Them Away

The next example is a particularly good one, I think, and adds another slightly trickier dimension to this kind of clue. All the required elements of a good anagram clue are here, and they are all connected to a painting and decorating theme, meaning that they work very cleverly together.

**Four coats spread over centre of ceiling
won't fade (10)**

Here 'spread' is the pointer that we need. We are being instructed to spread out the letters and mix them into an anagram. Assuming that we are to use the words 'four coats' (as the order of the wording in the clue is clearly directing us to do), there is an obvious problem – there are only nine letters to play with, and the solution requires ten.

So, let's take a closer look at the clue. What is at the centre of ceiling? Stop thinking about light fittings, ceiling roses or cracks, and concentrate on the word itself rather than its meaning. 'Ceiling' is a seven letter word, and at its centre is the letter L. What this clue is asking us to do is to mix up the letters of 'four coats' and then drop the added letter L somewhere into the middle, to find an answer that means 'won't fade'.

Solution: COLOURFAST

Here is a more complex example:

Section of turbulent sea area covered by opening and closing of curtain? (9)

Our pointer word here is 'turbulent', telling us to shake up and make an anagram of the words 'sea area', but that only gives us seven letters. So, what can we add? Look at the phrase 'opening and closing of curtain'? Here we are being told to take the opening and closing letters, i.e. the first and last letters of 'curtain', which are C and N, and add them to our anagram of 'sea area', so we now have the required nine letters to play with. In fact, the word 'covered' even tells us where specifically to put these two letters – C at the start and N at the end, so they are 'covering' the other seven. Quite a tricky solution to work out, with all those vowels, and not the most obvious meaning of 'section' either, but

that's what cryptic crosswords are all about – looking
beyond the obvious to discover the devious.

Solution: CAESAREAN

In the same way that extra letters can be added to an
anagram, so they can just as easily be taken away. Take a
look at this example:

Doctor desperate when rate drops – this rate? (5)

The word 'doctor' is often used as an anagram pointer,
asking us to doctor the word that follows. So, 'desperate'
provides us with our anagram letters, but there are nine
of them – and that's too many! Next we are told that
'rate drops'. So, let's drop the letters R, A, T and E from
our anagram word. What we have left are the five letters
we need to rearrange to find our answer: D, E, S, P and
E. And it has to mean another kind of 'rate'. Easy when
you know how!

Solution: SPEED

Finding Pointers

In the examples above, we have seen several pointer
words and phrases that may be used in cryptic
crossword clues to indicate an anagram:

*mix-up, new, disturb, reconstructed, revolutionary,
shattered, in a storm, somehow, spread, turbulent,
doctor.*

Each of these manages, in its own way, to tell us that the
letters within a word or phrase are to be broken, mixed,

re-arranged, confused or otherwise jumbled together.

There are hundreds more such words and phrases favoured by crosswords compilers, so no list can ever be exhaustive and you will have to keep your eyes and minds open to the many devious possibilities on offer. However, here, in no particular order, are just a few of the others you might come across:

transported, translated, diverted, treated, in order, out of order, not working, out of place, unusually, bursting, after refreshment, change, cocktail, playing, upset, collapse, arranged, re-arranged, arrangement, organised, dancing, in trouble, funny, bananas, crazy, bats, fancy, wrecked, make, made, Harry, wounded, crash, liquid, wild, trained, peculiarly, derelict, duff, fixed, twisted, rioting, after a fashion, working, struggling, wandering, vandalised, busy, badly, at sea, maybe, perhaps, move, exercises, cultivated, destruction, unsettled, confused, melee, untidy, played, worried, in distress, misled, damaged, different, possibly, deciphered, for a change, shuffled, managed, spoiled, wobbles, cooked, went off, crooked, exploded, bumpy, devastated, scatty, wasted, controversial, hectic, gibberish, exotic

4 The Answer's in the Question!

Another very straightforward and popular clue type, especially in many of the easier crosswords, involves nothing more than searching for the answer in its entirety right there in the wording of the clue. It may be quite cleverly hidden, or straddle several words, but you don't even have to mix the letters up. Just open your eyes and find it!

LOOKING FOR HIDDEN WORDS

Recognising the Signs

So, how do we know that this is what is required? How can we spot an 'answer in the question' clue? Just as in anagrams, we can expect three parts to the clue:

1. There will be a pointer – a word or two to hint that the answer is included in the wording of the clue and is therefore probably staring you in the face!

2. There will be a word or series of words in which the answer is hidden.

3. There will again be a word or phrase to tell you the meaning of the answer you are looking for.

Here's a very easy clue to show you what I mean:

Relationship is concealed during operation (5)

Our pointer here is the word 'concealed'. It is telling us that the answer we seek is hidden in the clue. In this example, it has something to do with 'relationship' and is hidden in the word 'operation'.

Solution: RATIO

Some Examples Explained

In the following more complex examples, the answer each time is spread over two words in the clue, so may not be so immediately clear:

Snake concealed in skimpy thong (6)

This clue is constructed on very similar lines to the first one, and even uses the same pointer word 'concealed'. Here we can see that there must be a word meaning 'snake' hidden in the phrase 'skimpy thong.' Don't get put off by the space between the words. Even though the answer here is hidden within a two-word phrase rather than in a single word, it is still there in its entirety, with all the letters in the right order, and remains relatively easy to spot.

Solution: PYTHON

Type of house millions live in (4)

The pointer that lets us know the type of clue this time is an even more obvious word than 'concealed' – it's the very simple 'in'. Can you spot a type of house hidden in

the wording of the clue? Again, ignore the spaces
between the words.

Solution: SEMI

Afternoon nap in Maisie's tavern (6)

Our pointer here is again the word 'in'. In this example,
we are looking for a word meaning 'afternoon nap' and
will find it in the two-word phrase 'Maisie's tavern'.
Again, ignore the space between the words, and don't be
confused by the presence of the apostrophe, or of any
commas, question marks or even full stops that might
turn up in similar clues. Learn to ignore punctuation.
Pretend it isn't there. Just find the right sequence of
letters and you will have your answer.

Solution: SIESTA

Here's another similar clue:

Speak highly of contents of next Olympics (5)

The pointer here is the word 'contents' which lets us
know that our answer is contained within the phrase
'next Olympics'. So we are looking for a five letter word
meaning 'speak highly', and again the answer is split
between two words. Remember the rule about taking no
notice of spaces and punctuation. It applies to capital
letters too. Ignore them.

Solution: EXTOL

Just occasionally, there will be no obvious pointer. The
clue is so short that there is no room, or even any real
need, for one. Look at this example:

Napoleon's star sign? (3)

There is an implication that the answer may be hidden in the word 'Napoleon' – if the sign is his, then it is probably there contained within his name – and the experienced crossword puzzler will spot that straightaway. Sometimes, knowing something like that will simply come with experience, but when it does crop up, the very short nature of the answer means it is likely to be a very easy one to spot anyway. And the sign in question here turns out to be an astrological sign – not perhaps the sort of sign you were expecting.

Solution: LEO

Finding pointers

Just as in the long list of possible anagram 'pointers' we saw in the previous chapter, there are lots of different ways a crossword compiler is able to indicate that a clue is of the 'answer hidden in the question' type. Here are a few words and phrases to consider, but there are many other possibilities:

in, inside, has, part of, a bit, within, contained, hide, hidden, concealed, central, shelters, guards, includes, protects, harbours, grasps, includes, retains, smothered, absorb, engulf, content, collect, selection . . .

USING ALTERNATE LETTERS

A little trick that crossword compilers may sometimes play is to use a variation of this type of clue – one where the answer is still hidden within the question, but the letters are not necessarily adjacent to each other. Now all we need to do is to pick out alternate letters to find the answer.

Recognising the Signs

The signs for this type of clue are similar to those above, but the pointer can be a little more subtle and sneaky. Here's an example:

Chain occasionally in prison (3)

What the 'answer in the question' clue type would normally lead us to expect would be to find either a word meaning 'chain' hidden in the word 'prison', or a word meaning 'prison' hidden in the word 'chain'. Neither of these exists here, but then there is no obvious pointer word to alert us to this being that type of clue, is there?

What we do have instead is the word 'occasionally'. We might spot our answer if we look at occasional or alternate letters instead of a straightforward reading of letters all in a row. Read the alternate letters in both the words 'chain' and 'prison', trying out both the odd and the even ones, and the answer will suddenly become clear. The answer is still there in the clue, but not so immediately obvious until we work out what we are expected to do.

Solution: CAN

Some Examples Explained

Here are another two 'alternate letters' clues as examples of how it's done:

Sold one odd fruit (4)

'Odd' is our pointer here, telling us not only that we are looking for alternate letters but that it's the odd, not the even, letters that will help us. So, it's letters numbered 1, 3, 5 and 7 of the phrase 'sold one' that will give us our four-letter answer – a kind of fruit.

Solution: SLOE

Man perhaps insulted now and then (4)

The pointer here is the phrase 'now and then' – another way of telling us to look only at alternate letters. Although we are not told whether it's to be the odd or even letters this time, it is clear that we are to look at alternate letters within the eight-letter word 'insulted' to find the answer. And there it is! Not the type of 'man' you probably expected, but that's the art of the cryptic clue – making you think laterally, throwing in the occasional unexpected meaning and requiring a small degree of general knowledge, in this case of geography.

But why is the word 'perhaps' there in the clue? This is a word often used to indicate an anagram, but not on this occasion. It is there simply because Man is just one example of an isle, but not the only one. So – perhaps Man, or perhaps some other island? The clue could as easily have said 'Man or Wight perhaps', but that would have given the game away, and really wouldn't have worked to deceive us quite so well, would it?

Solution: ISLE

Finding Pointers

So, the alternate letter clues have their own vocabulary of pointer words and phrases too. Here, including those we have looked at above, are just a few of the many possibilities:

> *occasionally, odd, now and then, alternate, once in a while, oddly, even, evenly, not every, taking turns, regularly, in odd places…*

INITIALLY SPEAKING

Another variation is where we are required to seek out just the initial letters of certain words within the clue. The answer is still hidden there in the clue, but just a little harder to find!

Recognising the Signs

These clues are usually quite easy to recognise. There will always be a pointer to let you know it's just the first letters you are looking for. The following example demonstrates one of these pointers in action.

Sister wipes a baby initially using this? (4)

Notice here that the answer is hidden in the clue, but the letters cannot be read consecutively. The pointer is 'initially' – a pretty clear indication that we are to look just for initial letters. Take the first letters of each of those first four words and we find what sister uses for her task!

Solution: SWAB

Some Examples Explained

And now we move on to look at some more of the other possible 'initial letters' pointers that you may come across. This next clue also asks us to spot some initials and the pointer used here is 'first':

Fame in city of divorce (West Nevada's first) (6)

The divorce city is, of course, Reno, so a little general knowledge will come in handy for this one. And all we have to do then is add the W and the N to find our answer, meaning 'fame'.

Solution: RENOWN

Here is another. The pointer now is 'tops':

Crewmen are tops in Oxford Amateur Rowing Society (4)

Solution: OARS

In the next clue, the pointer is 'leads'. Some general knowledge may be needed to recognise the famous player, although finding his name is easy enough when the right initials are picked out:

Chess player's leads of king and rook produce overall victory (6)

Solution: KARPOV

And, lastly, a clue using yet another very obvious pointer, this time 'at the beginning':

Writer's blue ink ran out at the beginning (4)

Solution: BIRO

Finding Pointers

A shorter list this time, most of which we have seen in the examples above.

> *Initially, first, firstly, at the beginning, at the start, for starters, leads, heads, ahead, front, at the forefront, tops...*

5 Going Backwards

Many cryptic clues rely in some way on the clue itself, the answer, or just part of a clue or answer, having to be read in reverse.

READING WORDS IN REVERSE

Following on from the previous chapter's search for answers already hidden in the clue, there is another clever trick that often crops up, and that's hiding the answer the other way around – with the letters appearing in reverse within the clue. These are not always quite so easy to spot, but the principle is exactly the same. The answer is right there in front of you, perhaps even found in alternate letters as before, but it's back to front.

Recognising the Signs

As always, we can expect a pointer word that tells us to read and search in reverse, and a clear hint that tells us the meaning of our prospective answer. Then just look out for the answer among the remaining words of the clue, but this time by reading from right to left.

Here are two examples:

Poor family's partially swept-back hair-do (4)

Our pointer here is 'swept-back' – a very clear indicator that something is written backwards. 'Partially' tells us we are looking for our answer in just part of the clue (in other words, the answer is hidden somewhere within the clue). In this case 'poor family' will give us what we are looking for, but only if we search through its letters backwards, from right to left. Ignore any spaces as usual. The answer, of course, is going to be something that means 'hair-do'.

Solution: AFRO

Connive to take part in some dull occasion in recession? (7)

Our pointer phrase here is 'in recession'. The words 'part' and 'some' are also hinting that the answer is hidden in just part or some of the clue. Reading backwards, it shouldn't take long to spot the seven-letter word that means 'connive'.

Solution: COLLUDE

The Two-stage Clue

The answer to a reverse-word clue may not however always be visible in the question, as it is in the above examples. There are other ways a cryptic clue can take advantage of reversing techniques.

So now we come to a common trick beloved of crossword compilers – to make you solve the clue, or part of it, first – and then to reverse that answer.

Here's quite a clever little example:

Where to hide currency back in Iran? (4)

In this case, the word 'back' is hinting that something is to be read backwards – but what? The word 'hide' might well lead us to expect that the answer is hidden in the clue itself, but it is not. To solve this one, you will need a little knowledge of world currencies. The currency of Iran is called the RIAL. It is this word the clue is asking us to read 'back'. So, having solved stage one of the clue, we must now turn that answer around and read it from back to front to find a word giving us 'where to hide'.

So, we have to solve this particular clue in two separate stages to find our eventual answer. First, find out the currency of Iran, and then reverse it.

Solution: LAIR

There are many ways that techniques like this can operate, so here are a few more examples of how other crossword compilers might employ the reversing of words to useful effect:

Important people turned over wide boy (4)

'Turned over' is the pointer we need here. First we think of another word for important people (VIPs) and then, in the second stage of solving this clue, we reverse it to find our 'wide boy'. Is that a slang word? Perhaps it is, but it is commonly understood and in the dictionary, so there's nothing wrong with using it.

Solution: SPIV

Town not to cry over (6)

Here 'over' gives us our pointer that something has to be read backwards, and we are looking for a town as our answer. That leaves us with the words 'not to cry'. First we solve the part of the clue relating to cry. Another word with the same meaning is 'sob'. In the second stage of this clue, just reverse the words 'not' and 'sob' and we have the answer.

Solution: BOSTON

One hundred and one left climbing in hot place (6)

Obviously 'climbing' is our pointer here, although it does seem to imply an upward rather than a backward movement! In this case, we have to solve two separate parts of the clue before reversing them to get the solution.

Firstly, we need another way of saying 'one hundred and one'. 101 could be loosely translated as the letters I, O and I, but these do not usually appear consecutively in any English words, so a more likely way is by using Roman numerals – a common occurrence in crosswords, and one we will look at in more detail later on in this book. Then we need another way of saying 'left' – there are a few possibilities (abandoned, remaining, etc.) but, when it comes to crosswords, the nautical version is often the one required. On board a ship, the left is referred to as the port side. So, we have to put the Roman CI and the word 'port' together and then, in stage two, reverse them to find the eventual answer.

Solution: TROPIC

Finding Pointers

As usual, all clues that use some form of reversing technique need a pointer word to give us the hint we need. Here are just some of the ways we might be told that some part of the clue or the answer requires us to look at it in reverse:

back, backwards, reverse, in recession, over, up, upwards, rejects, flip, in a spin, turn, turned over, climbing, upside down, cartwheel, head over heels, reverting, returning, from the east, travelling west...

6 Now It's Your Turn

Now it's your turn to have a go at solving a few clues, based entirely on what we have learned in Chapters 3, 4 and 5. The following ten clues are a mixture of anagrams, answers hidden in the question, and various word-reversing techniques. There are no tricks, although some clues are quite cleverly devised.

In each case, look out for the pointer to determine which type (or types) of clue it is, and then try to solve it. Clues are arranged in approximate order of difficulty, easiest first. If you get stuck, a brief explanation appears alongside each solution

CLUES FOR PRACTICE

Clue 1: Keen interest shown in bronze statue (4)

Clue 2: All he does gets wasted in property (9)

Clue 3: Maybe a versatile content group of young scouts (7)

Clue 4: G. Brown picked up a fly (4)

Clue 5: It gives out light if mantle is not working (8)

Clue 6: He flew from Moldavia to Russia, central part only (7)

Clue 7: Gather up bucket (4)

Clue 8: Doctor retained item positioned in between (12)

Clue 9: Remove comma. It's out of place recalling the dead (13)

Clue 10: In odd places, prince played cool instrument (7)

The Solutions

Clue 1: ZEST

This is a short and easy to solve clue, with the answer hidden among the letters of the phrase 'bronze statue', ignoring the spaces between the words. The very simple pointer word is 'in' and the solution, of course, means 'keen interest'.

Clue 2: LEASEHOLD

A simple enough anagram of 'all he does' with 'wasted' as our pointer, and a solution that means a type of property.

Clue 3: BEAVERS

The pointer word 'content' lets us know that the answer is hidden inside (within the contents of) the question. Here again we have to ignore the spaces between words to find our answer buried in the phrase 'maybe a versatile'. Beavers are, of course, junior boy scouts, so a small amount of general knowledge is needed.

Clue 4: GNAT

Ignore the fact that G. Brown makes you think of a former Prime Minister – that is just a red herring. Here we have a simple two-stage clue, using a reversing technique. 'Picked up' is our pointer, telling us that we must reverse a word that means 'brown'. Solve that part of the clue first – 'tan' – and then reverse it, tacking it on to the existing letter G, and we have our fly!

Clue 5: FILAMENT

The pointer 'not working' tells us that some of the

words may be broken, so this is an anagram clue. And here we have a quite straightforward example, using the words 'if mantle'. I like the fact that the whole clue works together and makes sense, with everything in it being lighting-related, in a similar way to the 'colourfast' clue with its decorating connotations that we looked at in Chapter 3.

Clue 6: AVIATOR
Who flew? Remember that this is a cryptic, not a general knowledge crossword, so don't be tempted to try to find out which historical figure may have taken such a trip! Here, the phrase 'central part only' gives a very clear indication that the answer is hidden in the centre of 'Moldavia to Russia'. Ignore the spaces and, from there, it's an easy step to finding the solution.

Clue 7: TEEM
The shortest words are not always the easiest to solve! The pointer 'up' leads us to something in reverse, but what? There is no four-letter word here to turn around, so this is obviously a clue that expects us to solve stage one, find that answer, and then reverse it. So, we want a four-letter word that means 'gather' one way round, and 'bucket' when read in reverse. The word 'bucket' instantly makes us think of water containers, doesn't it? But once you figure out that PAIL is just not right, there is no option but to look for another meaning. When it buckets down with rain...

Clue 8: INTERMEDIATE
'Doctor' is a very commonly used pointer to tell us we

are dealing with an anagram, and this is a particularly long example, using the twelve letters of the phrase 'retained item' to come up with something meaning 'positioned in between'. It would have been easy to spot the word 'retained' and assume that was a pointer to an 'answer in the question' type of clue, but hopefully you were not fooled by this small red herring for too long!

Clue 9: COMMEMORATIVE

Don't be fooled by all those instructions in the clue about punctuation! And, although 'recalling' might cleverly mislead you into thinking that something has to be read in reverse, this is actually just an anagram of 'remove comma it', pure and simple, with 'out of place' being the only pointer we need to set us on the right path to finding what it is that might help us to recall the dead.

Clue 10: PICCOLO

This clue is a nice mixture of two types. It's partly looking for alternate letters hidden in the question (P, I and C being alternate letters found in the word 'prince') and partly an anagram (COOL = C O L O). So, we have two pointers – 'in odd places' for the first part, and 'played' for the second. Solve both parts, and then simply tack them together to find the instrument required.

7 Double Meanings

The English language is full of words and phrases that have more than one meaning, and these provide great ammunition for crossword compilers in their attempts to trick you.

WORDS WITH TWO OR MORE MEANINGS

Let's take a look at a few simple everyday examples. The word 'fair' can as easily mean 'blonde' as it does 'fete' or even 'just'. And 'lay' could make you think of chickens laying eggs, preachers who are non-clergy, placing something down (like a head on a pillow), laying the table with cutlery, or even an old-fashioned song!

Recognising the Signs

Crossword compilers certainly play on these double meanings, using all manner of tricks that revolve around words having more than one meaning or those that do not necessarily mean what you are led to think they do. But don't expect a pointer word for these clues. Your only way of recognising them may simply be the fact that there appear to be two otherwise unconnected parts to the clue or that two meanings are implied in the wording. Look at this clue, for instance:

Move text up and down in old manuscript (6)

All you have to do here is find a word that means 'move text up and down' and that also means 'old manuscript.' It doesn't matter if your words are nouns, verbs or adjectives, so long as they mean different things but are spelt in exactly the same way. So, this type of clue is really just testing the breadth of your vocabulary and, to some extent, your general knowledge – and the broader the better! In fact, you could probably get away with answering it using just one of the definitions, with the second providing useful but non-essential back-up. I like this particular clue as its two parts connect together well, with an answer that gives us the modern computerised method and the ancient way of studying a piece of writing.

Solution: SCROLL

Some Examples Explained

Here's a very simple example, this one relying on the use of a slang word:

Mix in prison (4)

One word that can mean either 'mix' or 'prison'? Easy! And there is no reason why crosswords can't use slang words (or informal words, as the dictionary may call them), just as long as they are in common enough use, and are actually in the dictionary.

Solution: STIR

This next clue is even simpler:

Landlady's character (6)

Just two words to play with this time, so there can be no ambiguity. Find the word that can mean either 'landlady' or 'character' and you've cracked it!

Solution: LETTER

And what could be simpler than a one-word clue?

Intercity? (4)

No, it has nothing to do with railways. Try separating the word into two parts, consider another meaning for the word 'inter' and all becomes clear.

Solution: BURY

A very common trick played by crossword compilers is to try to mislead you with the word 'flower', as in the following short clue:

Russian flower (5)

Do you know any Russian flowers? Probably not. This may look like a straightforward general knowledge question, but no, it's cryptic, and here the word 'flower' has nothing to do with botany. It's rivers that flow, and what we are seeking here is actually a Russian river! Remember this particular double meaning trick, as it crops up time and time again.

Solution: VOLGA

Here is another 'double meaning' clue, and this time it really does rely on your having a little geographical knowledge of Eastern Europe:

Divided city in Croatia (5)

Are we really expected to know which of Croatia's cities is divided? Of course not! But it is useful to know that Split is actually a Croatian city, and we also know that the same word (without its capital letter) has a second meaning too, and that's what confirms our answer.

Solution: SPLIT

Here's another clue that cleverly uses two meanings:

Carry better system (4)

Of course 'better' here is not used in the expected superlative sense, but refers to a national computerised system used by 'betters' (gamblers) and known as 'The Tote', so a little lateral thinking is needed. But the other meaning of 'tote' – to carry – is straightforward enough, and you might well solve this clue on the strength of that meaning alone if gambling is not your speciality.

Solution: TOTE

And while we are on a betting theme:

Top singer's risky bet (6)

Here we have two very different meanings of the same word, and again both are spelt in exactly the same way.

Solution: TREBLE

And here is another one that requires a small amount of general knowledge, this time of English literature:

He's behind character in Shakespeare play (6)

So simple, it doesn't really need any further explanation, does it?

Solution: BOTTOM

Finding Pointers

Hoping for pointers? Not this time! There is no clear foolproof way to spot these double meaning clues, and no obvious pointers in any of the above examples. But perhaps more than any other clue type, the double meaning clue is all about words – knowing what they mean, looking for the connection that words with very different meanings might have in common, and testing and expanding your vocabulary. What a great excuse to dip into the delights of the dictionary!

8 Sounds Familiar

The next type of clue we are going to explore is very similar to the double meaning clue, but instead of looking for two words that are spelt and pronounced in the same way but have different meanings, now we are looking for two words (or more) that have different meanings and are spelt differently, even though they sound exactly the same.

WHAT IS A HOMOPHONE?

Confused? Think of hair and hare, bear and bare, would and wood. Sound familiar? Then you will know what I mean. Each of these words, spelt differently, and sounding just the same as another while having a totally different meaning, is known as a homophone. Homophones are a very handy device that crossword compilers make use of regularly, and often very cleverly.

Recognising the Signs

This clue type will almost certainly need to include a hint, or a pointer, to guide us towards the solution – something that lets us know we are listening to the sound of the words rather than taking notice of their spelling.

Try this easy clue which uses the word 'say' as its pointer:

Agreement is in the bag, say (4)

Just as in the double meaning clues in the previous chapter, here we are looking for a word that means two different things: both 'agreement' and 'in the bag.' In fact, in a clue like this, it is actually two words we seek – two distinctly different words that just happen to sound the same, even though they will be spelt differently.

This type of clue certainly needs a little lateral thinking, and a mental sweep of your known vocabulary, comparing possible words until you find the two that sound identical while managing to match both meanings. Here you should arrive at 'pact' and 'packed', and will have to choose the first of these as your answer as it is the only one that fits the 4-letter space in the crossword grid.

Solution: PACT

Some Examples Explained

The next clue works in the same way:

Sterilised one of the pack, we hear (6)

Here we need to find two words that sound the same but can mean either 'sterilised' or 'one of the pack'. Again, the two answers will not be spelt in the same way. They just sound the same – and 'we hear' is the pointer that leads us to that conclusion. 'Sterilised', of course, can mean pure or extra clean, but here it is being used in the medical or veterinary context. There is a little trickery going on, with that vet reference tending to make us think of animal packs, but don't be misled. Think beyond the obvious. The pack we want here is actually a pack of cards.

So our solution could be either 'spayed' or 'spade' – both sounding exactly the same. But the answer is six letters long, so it's easy to decide which word is required.

Solution: SPAYED

Here's another example:

Uniform fabric needed for ignition, some might say (5)

Again, we have a clear pointer – 'some might say'. So what two words that sound the same can mean both 'uniform fabric' and something 'needed for ignition'? Once you have made the connection – khaki and car key – it is clear which of the two possible words is the answer needed, simply by its 5-letter length. Note here also that 'car key' is actually two words, so short phrases do crop up in this type of clue from time to time.

Solution: KHAKI

I like this next rather clever clue, which again employs a two-word phrase as one of its possible 'sound-alikes':

Medicine that brought you and I together, we hear (7)

There is a particularly ingenious connection here

between our two possible meanings, with 'linctus' and 'linked us' sounding uncannily alike. Again, it's the number of letters that tells us which to choose as the answer.

Solution: LINCTUS

Here's one that requires a little specialist knowledge, this time of well-known playwrights:

Put a tick against Russian playwright, say (5,3)

The easiest way to tackle this one may well be to work your way through a few Russian playwrights and say them aloud until you find one that sounds like, and therefore matches, the other required meaning. Or you might go about it the other way around, searching for a two-word phrase that means 'put a tick against' until you find an answer that sounds like the name of a playwright. Either way, as soon as you have a match, the clue is solved.

Solution: CHECK OFF

This next clue is a little tenuous, relying on both a colloquial or slang term and a 'sound-alike' that doesn't actually sound absolutely identical. Nevertheless, it appeared in a national newspaper crossword:

BBC releases, say, 'What vehicles need in winter' (10)

The pointer is, again, 'say' – probably the most commonly used for this type of clue. So, do you know what the BBC's nickname is? Yes, it's 'Auntie'. Another word for 'releases' is 'frees' – so when you put the two parts together, you will find the answer. But does 'anti' actually sound the same as 'Auntie'? I'm not so sure. Perhaps it does if you say it in an American accent! But we have to remember that it's all just a bit of fun, so does it matter anyway, as long as we have managed to solve the clue?

Solution: ANTIFREEZE

And then we have to consider how to deal with the problem that occurs when your two sound-alike words are both the same length, as in this clue:

Put it down on paper, OK? (5)

Quite an easy one to solve, but which of the two possible answers is the one we want? When both have the same number of letters, as here, it is not always possible to decide which is the answer until you have found some of the letters of the answer, and you can only do this by solving at least one other interlocking clue. As soon as you discover, for instance, that the fourth letter of the answer must be an H, it will become obvious which of the two words to choose.

Solution: WRITE or RIGHT

Finding Pointers

When it comes to pointers for the 'sounds familiar' clue type, there is quite a varied list, with many other possibilities that I have probably either forgotten or have yet to come across, but here are just a few to consider:

sound, by the sound of it, say, some say, it's said, heard, we hear, hearing, on the tongue, state, stated, overheard, picked up, broadcast, aired . . .

9 Letter Maths

What I mean by 'Letter maths' is basic addition and subtraction. This type of clue requires you to add or take away certain letters to find your answer. It's a kind of sum done using words instead of numbers. We have already seen a couple of examples of how this might be achieved in Chapter 3, where extra letters had to be added to, or removed from, the letters of an anagram word before mixing them all up to find the answer.

SUBTRACTION

Let's start with taking letters away, as this is a very commonly used crossword device. One or more letters either have to be taken from a word or phrase in the clue, removed from an anagram word before jumbling the letters up, or even taken from the answer itself. Let's find out how.

Recognising the Signs

Just as in many other clue types, you are likely to be given a pointer that tells you what to do – in this case hinting at the need to remove certain letters. Words like 'lose' or 'drop' are common examples. (There is a list of many others on page 71.) But compilers of cryptic crosswords can be cunning, and often you will first have to solve at least part of the clue before being able to remove a letter or letters from your answer – another case of the 'two-stage' clue we talked about in Chapter 5 where an answer had to be found before we were able to reverse it.

Take a look at this example:

Kent port lost lead and is finished (4)

Being told that the 'lead' is lost means we have to lose, or take away, the leading (first) letter. So, first we need to find a Kent port five letters long, so we can then remove the first letter to arrive at a four-letter answer meaning 'finished'. Whether you work your way through a list of ports or go straight to thinking of alternative words for 'finished' is up to you. The port we want here, of course, is Dover.

Solution: OVER

Some Examples Explained

In the above clue, we were told precisely which letter to remove – the first. In the next clue, it's the last.

Sea bird's nearly out of breath (6)

If you are out of breath, you are likely to be puffing. And if you are 'nearly' puffing, we can assume that it's not quite the whole word that we are after, so its ending has to be lost. With a hint of double meaning going on here, and even a touch of the 'sounds familiar' technique too, our answer, having dropped its last letter, becomes a sea bird – a puffin.

Solution: PUFFIN

And here is another that clearly expects us to remove the last letter:

Platform for flower with no root (4)

There is a huge temptation here to think the 'flower' is bound to be a river. After all, it's a well-used trick, as discussed in an earlier chapter. But sometimes, especially in the less complicated crosswords, we can just take things at face value. This is a genuine flower (daisy), losing its last letter (or 'root') to leave us with a word meaning platform.

Solution: DAIS

Rather than pointing you towards removing a first, last or even middle letter, some clues may target a particular letter of the alphabet as the one to be taken away, as in this example:

One left country, wanting food (6)

Being told to remove 'one' from the name of a country could very easily lead you to assume that it is the letter I that has to be removed. In fact, it is an A. If you have one ball, for example, then you have a ball, so the word 'a' is often used in crosswords to mean 'one'. The country, of course, is Hungary, and removing the letter A from it leaves us with our 'wanting food' answer.

Solution: HUNGRY

And here we are being asked to remove the letter N:

American's forgotten name of cattle (3)

The American is, of course, a YANK, and we are removing the letter N (a commonly used abbreviation for 'name') to reveal a kind of cattle. Our pointer here is the word 'forgotten' which is letting us know that the N is meant to go.

Solution: YAK

In this more complex clue, we are being asked to remove the letter H:

She used to run ward in Northam back when hospital was axed (6)

So clever! This clue not only asks us to take a specific letter of the alphabet away, but it also combines several of the other clue types we have looked at in previous chapters. By 'axing' or removing the H (a common abbreviation for 'hospital') from the word Northam, and then reversing what is left, we find our answer hidden in the clue. And just look at those three sneaky pointers: 'in' telling us that the answer is in the question, 'back' telling us to reverse a word, and 'axed' telling us to take a letter away!

Solution: MATRON

But latter maths clues aren't always quite so helpful. They don't always tell you which letter or collection of letters is to be subtracted. Sometimes, although the pointer is there to tell you to take something away, it's up to you to work out which of the letters have to go. Here's an example:

Postman drops three letters leaving Arab country (4)

The pointer is obvious, but which three letters are we supposed to drop from the word 'postman' to leave us with the country we need? Just try experimenting. With only seven letters to play with, it won't take long to reach the answer, and there is no indication that we have to mix the letters up, so they are likely to appear in the right order.

Solution: OMAN

This next clue is deceptively simple, but we first have to work out for ourselves which letter of the alphabet is to be removed:

Lots of anonymous pasta? (6)

If something or someone is anonymous, it has no name. The word 'name' in crossword-speak is often abbreviated to the letter N as we saw in the YAK clue above. So, just think of a type of pasta (here it turns out to be noodles), and remove the letter N, leaving an answer that means 'lots.'

Solution: OODLES

And, in this final example, it's half a word we have to remove!

Chose work over tedium, not half! (5)

'Op' is a common abbreviation meaning 'work' (Latin: opus), and crops up in crosswords time and time again. Now all we have to do is take away half (three letters) of the word 'tedium' before finding the answer, which means 'chose'. Which half? Experiment with the possibilities, put them after 'op' and it's not too hard to work that one out.

Solution: OPTED

Finding Pointers

As usual, these are just a few of the many possibilities you might come across, but it is by no means a definitive list:

lose, lost, drop, take, taken, take-away, go, depart, leaving, leaves, ignore, forget, forgotten, not, went away, left, abandoned, thrown out, evicted, most, almost, nearly, largely, mainly, not quite, not all there, cut off, axed, missing, gone, going, going away, without, runs out, disappear...

In some cases, the pointer also gives you a pretty good hint as to whereabouts in a word the subtraction has to be made. Here are some pointers that will help you to target specific letters or parts of the clue word:

first, beginning, opening, final, last, ends, finish off, unfinished, topless, headless, head off, bottomless, endless, rootless, tip, centre, middle, contents, half, quarter, any given fraction or percentage, shortened, non-stop, gutted, nonetheless (removing the letter O)...

ADDITION

Now let's move on to the matter of adding letters on rather than removing them. These don't seem to appear quite so regularly as the subtraction clues. Again, there are many ways this device can be used, but we will always be given pointers to help us decide what is required.

Recognising the Signs

Now we are looking for a clear hint that we are to add a letter, or more than one, to some aspect of the clue or solution. As usual, there are many ways this can be done, and the list of possible pointers at the end of the chapter may help. Try this simple example for starters:

Bear to hold end of rope and pull (5)

The 'end of rope' in this case of course means the last letter of the word 'rope' – and that's an E. So a word meaning 'bear' has to hold the letter E. In other words the letter E will appear somewhere in the middle, not at either of the ends, and our eventual solution will mean 'pull'. But don't be fooled into taking the obvious path. The 'bear' here is not an animal. Think of 'bear' in the sense of 'bearing a scar', and its link to 'have' becomes a lot clearer.

Solution: HEAVE

Some Examples Explained

The next three examples again point us towards a specific letter or group of letters found within the clue:

Can a chef possibly hold tin-opener? No hope! (3,6)

A clever mix of clue types, this one! The word 'possibly' is a common pointer to an anagram. Mixing up the words 'Can a chef' won't quite do it though – we are still a letter short. So, let's employ a little letter maths. What letter are we being asked to add to the mix? The opening letter to 'tin', of course, and that's a T.

Solution: FAT CHANCE

Chatter with religious leader, first in temple (6)

Take the first letter of 'temple' – it's the letter T again – and just add it to 'rabbi'. It's as simple as that! But notice the absence of a pointer. There is nothing specifically telling us to add. The letter T simply tacks on at the end and follows the rabbi to make the new word required, which means 'chatter'.

Solution: RABBIT

Middle East writer's tree (5)

This clue needs no specialist knowledge of Middle Eastern authors or plants. What it is telling us to do is to take the middle of 'East' – just the two letters AS – and add them to a writer. The writer here is not a specific author's name but simply a pen, and the result of adding the two elements of the clue together is the tree we are seeking.

Solution: ASPEN

Here's another to be thinking about:

East End priest trained expert at Aintree? (7)

The pointer 'trained' is telling us to make an anagram of the word 'priest', but that only gives us six letters. We need one more, and it's the East that features yet again. Quite cleverly, it is 'end' that provides the second pointer in this clue. It's the end letter of East that needs to be picked off this time, and added in front of the anagram letters. Because the two parts of the answer just sit side by side, we are not given a clear pointer as we might if the T was to be dropped somewhere into the middle. And why the question mark? Simply because Aintree is not the only possible racecourse, just as Man (in Chapter 4) was not the only isle.

Solution: TIPSTER

Adding Whole Words

Sometimes you will be required to add more than just a letter or two. A whole word may need to be placed either inside, around or next to another to create the answer. Here are a couple of examples:

Horse, high one, stabled by lad (8)

Here we are putting the whole word 'tall' (meaning 'high') together with an I to denote 'one' inside the word 'son' (an alternative for 'lad') to find our horse. The rather unusual pointer here is 'stabled' which is, of course, very apt given the subject matter of this particular clue.

Solution: STALLION

Firm admits a bad mistake somewhere in Las Vegas (6)

Our pointer word here is 'admits'. 'Co' is a very obvious abbreviation for 'company' or 'firm', and here it admits 'a sin' which is a pretty bad mistake!

Solution: CASINO

Finding Pointers

Here are just a few of the many 'addition' pointers you may come across:

add, in, inside, sent in, involved, included, hold, held, calling in, inviting, covers, adds, accepts, admits, eats, swallows, embraces, intervenes, suppresses, catching, controlling, stabled, incurring, next to, after, follows, before, besides…

MOVING AND REPLACING LETTERS

Letter maths can go beyond simply adding letters or taking them away. Another variation to this type of clue involves being asked to move letters around within a word, or to replace one or more letters with others.

Some Examples Explained

Here are a few examples:

Runners smooch back to front (4)

Beware! 'Back to front' is going to mislead you down the reversal route. But this one is a little more subtle. It's not the whole word we are going to read in reverse this time. In fact, what this clue is telling us to do is to take the letter at the back of a word and move it to the front. We know it is four letters long. The most obvious alternative four-letter word for 'smooch' is 'kiss'. And when we move its final letter to the front, we find the answer.

Solution: SKIS

News articles I'd sent in instead of Henry (7)

This clue wants us to remove the H for Henry from a word meaning 'articles' and replace it with the letters ID. As ever, the apostrophe, like all punctuation, can be ignored. I will tell you that the articles here are 'things'. Now do the maths. The answer, of course, means 'news'.

Solution: TIDINGS

I left centre for university, causing confusion (6)

A simple replacement is needed here. U for university replaces the letter I which has left. So, just find another word meaning centre (try 'middle'), then do the required maths.

Solution: MUDDLE

Order peach melba with it ignoring me?
That's another order (10)

This starts out as an anagram of 'peach melba' ('order' being our pointer), but first we have to do some maths – adding the letters IT and taking away the letters ME. Only now will the mixed-up letters give us another kind of 'order' altogether!

Solution: ALPHABETIC

Finding Pointers

These pointers make it pretty clear that a movement or replacement of one or more letters is necessary, and often tell you exactly where to make the change too. Here are a few examples:

instead, back to front, takes place, trading places, first to last, opening to closing, stands in, substitutes, top to toe…

10 Now It's Your Turn

Now it's your turn to have another go at solving a few clues, this time based on what we have learned in Chapters 7, 8 and 9. The following ten clues are a mixture of double meanings, sounds familiar and letter maths clues. There are no tricks, although some clues are quite cleverly devised.

In each case, look out for the pointer to determine which type (or types) of clue it is, and then try to solve it. Clues are arranged in approximate order of difficulty, easiest first. If you get stuck, a brief explanation appears alongside the solutions.

MORE CLUES FOR PRACTICE

Clue 1: Release without charge (4)

Clue 2: Junior doctor picked up one after another (2,4)

Clue 3: Start up without a meal (5)

Clue 4: Stop talking. The engagement's over (4,3)

Clue 5: Place to put bowler that doesn't start to fight (3,3)

Clue 6: Courage and audacity in jam (10)

Clue 7: Number leave side, getting strong criticism (4)

Clue 8: What rugby forwards do helps to improve the skin (4,4)

Clue 9: Topless flower girls catch cold. Snobs snub them (5,7)

Clue 10: Suffer punishment or accept non-stop therapy (4,3,3)

The Solutions

Clue 1: FREE
This is a very simple double meaning clue which I hope requires no further clarification.

Clue 2: IN TURN
Here the pointer 'picked up' should alert us to the fact that this is a sounds familiar type of clue. We are looking for two sound-alike words or phrases which are spelt differently – one that means a junior doctor (intern) and the other that means one after another (in turn). As we need a two-word answer, we will choose the latter.

Clue 3: LUNCH
A simple letter maths clue, where 'without' is the pointer towards a subtraction. Once you have solved stage 1, by finding a 6 letter word meaning start up ('launch'), you just have to take away the letter A.

Clue 4: RING OFF
Straightforward double meanings!

Clue 5: HAT BOX
This is quite a clever clue, combining simple letter maths (subtracting the first letter of the word 'that') and a double meaning, where the word 'box' can mean two different things – a container or to fight. Even the possible double meaning of the word 'bowler' could throw you off the trail in search of a cricketing answer rather than one about a hat!

Clue 6: BOTTLENECK

No, not strawberry jam! There are several double meanings going on here. Courage, in slang terms, is bottle. Audacity, also in slang, is neck. Put the two together and you get the kind of jam that might occur in traffic.

Clue 7: FLAK

Another letter maths example. The letter N (short for 'number') has to leave. So, first look for a 5-letter word meaning 'side'. Try 'flank'. Then just drop the letter N.

Clue 8: FACE PACK

This is a double meanings clue. As usual for this type, there is no pointer word, but we are given two parts to the clue which have no obvious connection with each other. What on earth can rugby moves and skin preparations have in common? The two words we are looking for have a double meaning and are able to answer both questions.

Clue 9: LOWER CLASSES

The flower here is not a river, which might have been your first thought if you have remembered one of crosswords' most common teasers. No, it's the word 'topless' here which is the giveaway. We are simply being asked to subtract the first letter from the word 'flower'. So that gives us the first word of our answer. The girls we need in our second word are, of course, lasses. Then just 'catch' the letter C (a common abbreviation for 'cold') by putting it between the two words, and the answer becomes clear.

Clue 10: TAKE THE RAP

Here it is 'non-stop' that tells us the word 'therapy' is not quite complete – that it has lost its final letter. Once we have worked that one out, the rest becomes easy.

11 Keeping It Short

Now we come to abbreviations. The best dictionaries and crossword companions carry long lists of them, and many will be instantly familiar anyway, so it's really not practical or necessary for me to try to list them all here.

ABBREVIATIONS COMMONLY USED IN CROSSWORDS

We have already encountered a few examples of commonly used one-letter abbreviations while looking at other clue types. N for example usually represents 'name' or 'number', H stands for 'hospital', and C might mean 'cold', or sometimes 'about' from the Latin 'circa'.

In cryptic crosswords, it is often necessary for a compiler to require the use of one, two or more extra letters for adding, subtracting, substituting etc. in anagrams and other clues. We have seen lots of examples when looking at letter maths techniques in Chapter 9. Abbreviations can provide many of these odd letters.

Some of the Compilers' Favourites

■ single letters substituted for a whole word, like the

examples above. Others include F for fellow or female, M for male, W for woman, L for lake or learner (student), G for good, V for victory or very, T for time, and U for university. U often gets used in clues to mean 'posh' or upper class too.

- commonly used abbreviations for Latin words or phrases, like e.g., i.e., re and etc.

- chemical symbols representing elements from the periodic table (e.g. FE for iron, PB for lead, or AG for silver). And OR (from heraldic origins) is often used to mean gold, as an alternative to the more technically correct AU.

- musical notations (e.g. F for loud, FF for very loud, P for soft or quiet).

- the well-known shortened versions of common words like company (co), doctor (dr), road (rd), street (st), station (stn), church (ch, CE or RC), record (LP or EP), exercise (PE or PT), advertisement (ad), public relations (PR), or P for parking.

- abbreviations for specific organisations (e.g. AA, TA, NUT or BBC).

- initials that represent countries or states, (e.g. UK, USA, NI or CAL). You may recognise some of the less obvious examples from their car registration plates or the letters that appear on athletes' vests – e.g. E for Spain or CH for Switzerland.

■ qualifications or titles (e.g. MA, BSC, or the religious ones Rev, RR and DD).

■ abbreviations that stand for certain occupations (e.g. MD, MO, GP or MB all meaning doctor, SEN or SRN for nurse, Ed for editor, RA for artist, GI, RE or RA (again) for various kinds of soldier, or AB for Able Seaman or sailor).

■ times of the day, week or year (e.g. a.m., p.m., Mon, Tue, Jan, Feb, etc.). The letters D, W and Y can mean day, week and year, and WE is sometimes used as an abbreviation for weekend.

■ weights and measures (e.g. oz, lb, kg, ft, cc, ml, etc.).

■ Roman numerals, e.g. V (5), X (10), L (50), C (100), D (500) and M (1000). These are often used in combinations, like VI for 6, IV for 4, or XI for eleven, this last example often being used in clues to represent a team or side, as in football or cricket. K (as in kilo) and G (as in grand), although not Roman, can be used to mean 1000 too.

■ positional and directional words – L for left and R for right, and compass points N, S, W and E.

■ initials that represent royalty – K for King, Q for Queen, R for either Rex or Regina, and sometimes the initials for specific monarchs, e.g. VR for Victoria, or ER for our current queen.

■ truncated versions of words with apostrophes in them, like can't, won't, I'll or I'm.

There are many more possibilities and, to be honest, there is no easy way to learn and recognise them all, other than by experience and practice. Some of the more popular ones do make very regular appearances in cryptic clues, so it shouldn't take long to recognise them after a while.

Recognising the Signs

Don't expect pointers! You might be lucky and find the word 'short' or 'brief' to help you, but usually it's a case of working it out for yourself.

Some Examples Explained

Here are a range of different abbreviations being used in cryptic clues:

Talk about milliner (7)

A milliner is someone who makes hats – a hatter. Just add the letter abbreviation C, meaning 'about', and we get our word for talk.

Solution: CHATTER

All quiet in reservoir (4)

Another word for 'all' is 'sum', and here we are adding the letter P, an abbreviation in musical terms meaning 'quiet'.

Solution: SUMP

Controversial pioneer eats very soft pizza (9)

Even quieter or softer than P, we now have PP. This is another anagram clue, with 'controversial' as our pointer. Once you have jumbled up the seven letters of 'pioneer', they have to 'eat' or swallow up the two-letter abbreviation for very soft, to help us find our pizza.

Solution: PEPPERONI

Signal to warn pilot in old airline trick (6)

This one uses the abbreviated name of an airline which is no longer in existence (BEA) and joins it up with 'con' meaning a trick.

Solution: BEACON

Recommended intake does unusually contain silver (6)

The pointer 'unusually' tells us this is an anagram. So we mix up the four letters of DOES and then make sure they 'contain' the silver, which in this case is represented by the letters AG.

Solution: DOSAGE

Opportunity for women to host fashionable party (6)

A fashionable party is an 'in do', and it is hosted, meaning it is going to fall in the middle of the answer. So, who does the hosting? Here we see the abbreviation W representing woman, used twice – once at each end – and therefore meaning 'women' in the plural. The opportunity here, in modern language terms, is the resultant 'window'.

Solution: WINDOW

Melodramatic articles in Thailand, Rhode Island and California (10)

What a fantastic clue to illustrate some geographical abbreviations in action! The articles are, of course, the definite and indefinite articles in speech, 'the' and 'a', followed by three shortened versions of countries or states – T for Thailand, RI for Rhode Island, and CAL for California. Put them all together in that order and they make another word meaning 'melodramatic'.

Solution: THEATRICAL

Germany and America take time to clean up (4)

Another clue using abbreviations for countries, this one takes the D for Germany (Deutschland) and the US for America, and adds them to T, the commonly used abbreviation for 'time.'

Solution: DUST

Caretaker rejects rubbish after first day of year (7)

The pointer word 'rejects', as we saw in Chapter 5, is one of many possible indicators that something must be read in reverse. Here it's the rubbish or 'rot' that goes backwards, preceded by the abbreviated form of the first day of the year – which is Jan 1.

Solution: JANITOR

Old boy fills untidy drawer. He keeps suits in it (8)

The pointer 'untidy' tells us this is an anagram. You can mix up the six letters of 'drawer' but you still need two more letters, meaning 'old boy,' to fill the empty space in the middle. OB is a common abbreviation for 'old boy', often used in the names of school organisations and sports teams for ex-pupils.

Solution: WARDROBE

Cambridge college supports volunteers' income (7)

Still on a school or college theme, here we have the name of a specific Cambridge University college (Kings), preceded by the abbreviation TA, which stands for Territorial Army, who are volunteer soldiers.

Solution: TAKINGS

Track that is a help to rock band (6)

A track is a road. Now we just have to add 'that is' which, of course, is shortened down to i.e., as in the Latin term 'id est', before finding out who helps the band.

Solution: ROADIE

Rambler holds record for peace (6)

The rambler here is a rose, and the record it holds is the now outdated abbreviation EP, which in the days of vinyl records stood for extended play.

Solution: REPOSE

Imagine five hundred sheets of paper (5)

This clue uses the Roman numeral D to represent 500, and adds it to the ream of paper.

Solution: DREAM

A similar clue, using an alternative Roman number, might well have said:

One hundred sheets of paper are the best (5)

Solution: CREAM

Bear up with top lady in Arts Centre (6)

Just combine the word 'up' with the top lady, who is of course none other than the queen herself (ER), and put both inside the central two letters of Arts (RT) to find the bear in question.

Solution: RUPERT

As far as this chapter about abbreviations goes, I have decided to save the best until last. Although this next example is very much a 'going backwards' clue, with the word 'back' as the pointer, this is also a wonderful example of abbreviations in use – three of them in all.

Go wild! Knock out Manchester United's right back (3,4)

Just read the solution in reverse and see how clever this clue is! 'Knock out' is abbreviated to KO, the name of the team to Man U, and right to R.

Solution: RUN AMOK

12 Looking Out for Foreign Words

Many crosswords make use of the occasional foreign word or phrase. Naturally, you will not be expected to know any language other than English in any real depth, but a few examples do crop up quite regularly.

WORDS FROM OTHER LANGUAGES

The most commonly used words are likely to be French, although an awareness of the Greek alphabet always comes in handy too.

Recognising the Signs

This should be easy. It would be unusual for a crossword compiler to expect you to know that a foreign word was needed without actually telling you so in fairly plain terms. So, just look out for the words 'overseas' or 'abroad', 'French' (or 'in France') or 'Greek', or the occasional mention of another country or language. Sometimes just the name of a well-known foreign city is enough to point you to the language required.

French Words

The words most often used are the very simple two or three letter ones that many of us will recognise and understand, such as la, le or les, all meaning 'the'. Here is a simple example, which also makes use of two abbreviations:

Practical American sailor meets the French (6)

The American here is represented by the letters US, and the sailor by AB (both abbreviations already mentioned in Chapter 11). So all we need to add is one of the French words for 'the' – in this case it is 'le' – and our solution means 'practical'.

Solution: USABLE

Here's a clue that makes use of another short French word, meaning 'some':

Bed covering of some French animal doctor (5)

Even without knowing the French word here, you could probably work this one out, just by getting the word 'vet' and adding a couple of letters to find the rather obvious bed covering that is our answer.

Solution: DUVET

Now we move on to French numbers (probably only 1, 2 or 3), and specifically here to the French word, 'un'. This usually signifies either 'one' or 'a', as in this example which again combines more than one clue type:

In Paris, a girl ingests potassium?
It's inauspicious (7)

Although the word 'French' does not appear, 'in Paris' gives us a very similar pointer, and we will also need to call on our knowledge of chemical symbols (see Chapter

11) to know that potassium is abbreviated to K. Lucy is our girl's name here, although there is no way of knowing that for sure, other than looking for another word for 'inauspicious' and then working our way back to double-check that everything comes together and makes sense.

Solution: UNLUCKY

Although there will be other examples not covered here, one more small French word that does deserve a mention is 'rue' which means a street, road or way. It often crops up, and remember that the word 'rue' has other meanings in English – both regret and a specific type of plant or herb – so don't be surprised to find it in a double meaning context from time to time.

Going Beyond the French

In the following clue, no actual country or language is mentioned, but our pointer is 'overseas':

Wash three articles overseas? (7)

This is a clever little clue, asking us to find three different foreign words, each meaning an article, and then to sit them side by side to find the answer. So here we have 'la' from the French language, 'un' also from French, and 'der' from German.

Solution: LAUNDER

Sticking with German for a moment, here's a clue that uses the fairly well-known German word 'ich' meaning I. The pointer doesn't use the word German, but provided you know in which country Berlin lies, you should be okay!

In Berlin, I inhaled nitrogen, not very much (4)

Even in such a short clue, there is quite a lot going on here, with an abbreviation (N for nitrogen) and a little letter maths (as the N gets added or 'inhaled'), as well as the use of the foreign word.

Solution: INCH

The Greek Alphabet

Most dictionaries and crossword companions carry a full list of Greek letters, from alpha through to omega, so it's not necessary to know them in the right order or to remember them all by heart. Nevertheless, a few do appear quite regularly, and in time will start to become familiar to you. In most cases, all that's necessary is for you to spot the pointers that tell you a Greek letter is needed, so you can then check your list to find the right one.

Using F as an abbreviation for 'fine' and adding it to one of the letters of the Greek alphabet, this one should be easy to solve:

Fine Greek character's dairy product (4)

Solution: FETA

Here is another example, this time based on the 'letter maths' clue type:

In recent times, Greek character left stamp-collecting (6)

Here we are actually told that we need to find a Greek letter (or character). Knowing that he has 'left' should alert us to a letter maths subtraction. Provided you know that 'philately' is the proper name for stamp-collecting, it isn't too hard to take the Greek letter 'phi' away to arrive at our answer, which means 'in recent times'.

Solution: LATELY

The next clue also makes it perfectly clear that we are looking for a Greek letter, and this time makes use of two other clue types as well.

Greek character went first up the Acropolis initially (5)

Let's look at this one a stage at a time. 'Went first' is 'led' but the pointer word 'up' is telling us that we need to read this word backwards, so we get 'del'. Then we need some initials – that's what the second pointer word 'initially' is telling us. So, let's use the initial letters of the two words that follow: 'the Acropolis' or 'TA'. Put the two elements together, and we find our Greek letter – delta.

Solution: DELTA

Take a look at this final example (no pun intended!):

It's the last thing in home gadgets (5)

This is a 'hidden in the clue' type, so all we have to do is search among the letters, in the right order, to find the answer. What makes it a little more tricky is that we are not told this time that we are looking for a Greek letter. All we know is that our answer has to mean 'the last thing', and that is what Omega is – the last letter of the Greek alphabet.

Solution: OMEGA

13 A Little Knowledge Goes a Long Way

So, what do you already know, what can you find out, and what clues have you already solved that might help you to complete your crossword?

USING GENERAL KNOWLEDGE

Even cryptic clues can require some general, or even quite specialised, knowledge from time to time. Geography, history, royalty... It's definitely worth having internet access, or keeping a few reference or crossword companion books handy, particularly the kind that just provide you with useful alphabetical and word-length lists of composers, lakes, capital cities, currencies, etc. Usually, but not always, you will not actually need to know very much about the composer or lake in question!

You might also need some knowledge of world leaders, films, TV programmes, books, sportsmen, or a myriad of other random topics. There is no point in my offering detailed lists or suggestions here. There are just far too many possibilities!

Clues that Mix General Knowledge with Cryptic Elements

If clues were just straightforward general knowledge questions, they would not be appearing in a cryptic crossword. Here, some general knowledge will always be combined with some other cryptic element. Pointers can be vague, if present at all, but it is often fairly obvious in the wording of the clue that some knowledge is required. So, let's take a look at a few such clues in action:

One mad king's raised in country (6)

You could be forgiven for assuming that this clue is going to be an anagram ('mad' is a possible pointer), or that one of the usual abbreviations for a king (K or R) might be being deployed, but both these theories will just take you up a dead end. So, maybe it really is a king. 'Raised' is a good pointer that his name is to be read in reverse, and the 'one' can generally be taken to give us either a letter I or A. So, how many mad kings can you think of? This one comes from literature, so you may need to know your Shakespeare! Or you could take a different route and search your lists for six-letter countries beginning with I or A, and then find the name of the king by default.

Solution: ISRAEL

Staying with a literary theme, here's another clue that combines a couple of cryptic techniques to find the eventual solution:

Novelist and poet arranged to eat bread (8)

The pointer 'arranged' tells us there is an anagram involved, and that it is to be of the word 'poet'. 'Eats' implies a swallowing of other letters or a word inside the four re-arranged letters. Once we have figured out that we need four more letters as well as our anagram, 'roll' emerges as the likely bread in question, and Trollope as our novelist answer.

Solution: TROLLOPE

The next example again uses letter maths, this time in a two-stage clue:

Powerful US astronaut is disarmed (6)

First we need to find the name of a US astronaut, presumably a famous one. Then we need to remove the word 'arm' to find a solution meaning powerful. Once you have the name Armstrong, it's easy to see what is required.

Solution: STRONG

The next clue cleverly uses several cryptic techniques:

Book about Spanish golfer winning second of trophies (7)

In this one we can take the short word 're', much favoured by crossword compilers, to mean 'about'. The 'second of trophies' is pointing us towards using only the second letter of that word, i.e. the R. 'Winning' is a fairly loose kind of pointer, but what it is suggesting is that the golfer is to have the letter R included somewhere inside his name. So all we need now is our Spanish golfer. Perhaps the most famous of all was Seve Ballesteros. Combine 'Seve' with all these other elements, and the solution means 'book'.

Solution: RESERVE

This next clue is quite an easy one, with two halves to solve to 'make' the answer:

The pop singer over there might make Prime Minister (8)

'Over there' translates as 'that' and our pop singer is Cher. Together they make the name of one of our most famous PMs. But, if you are not well-up on your pop music or politicians, the clue could present more of a problem.

Solution: THATCHER

More Specialist Knowledge Required

Sometimes a fairly high level of inside knowledge is needed, and no amount of lists will help you, although an internet search can usually drag up something of assistance. In the next four examples, you do need to be very familiar with the subject matter in the clue in order to make sense of the quite specific references being made in them.

Shine – like Chopin? (6,6)

Quite a tricky problem, this one, if you know little about the composer Chopin! It may be best here to start with an open mind and just think cryptically. With two obvious sections to the clue, and no other pointers but the word 'like' to help you, this just could be a double meaning clue. So, let's concentrate on the 'shine' part and try to think of alternative phrases which might mean the same. After all, how many of us, unless we are classical music experts, are likely to know that Chopin was born in Poland but had a French father? Sometimes it is only through solving crosswords that we discover such information for the first time.

Solution: FRENCH POLISH

Grant film poster's within reach perhaps? (7)

Here we have an anagram of 'reach' – the pointer being 'perhaps'. And then some letter maths, as within the anagram we are being asked to put something meaning 'poster' – i.e. an advertisement, or 'ad'. So, why Grant? The word 'film' may help us towards working out that this is an actor. Not Hugh Grant, but Cary Grant, and the solution is going to be a 'Grant film', i.e. the name of a film he appeared in. Never heard of him, or the film? Never seen it? Perhaps you would need to do a little research, or perhaps just work it out from the cryptic elements and hope you have found the right answer. That's exactly what makes this particular kind of clue so tricky.

Solution: CHARADE

Massive star combines two roles in old cartoon (5,5)

To solve this one you will need to know about astronomy, and what term is used to describe a massive star, in particular. But you are also required to know your classic cartoons and, as it turns out, to recognise two of the characters from the Disney film *Snow White and the Seven Dwarfs*. Match the two and you have a rather clever answer, but without this level of knowledge, the clue could be a tricky one to solve.

Solution: WHITE DWARF

Stagger like Del Boy as chandelier finally dropped? (6)

If you have never watched *Only Fools and Horses*, this clue would be a complete mystery to you! But, assuming that you have seen the TV programme and recognise the Del Boy reference, you will probably also know that the character's surname is Trotter. Using one of the techniques we saw in Chapter 9, we now have to apply a little letter maths and 'finally drop', i.e. subtract the last letter of the word 'chandelier' (R), from the word 'Trotter' to find our answer, meaning 'stagger'. Of course, if you know the programme well, you will also appreciate the dropped chandelier reference which relates to a funny incident in one of the episodes, making this an even more satisfying clue.

Solution: TOTTER

USING PRIOR KNOWLEDGE

A final trick that often crops up in crosswords is to make use of what you have already worked out in one particular clue to help you to solve another clue in the same puzzle. Not so much general knowledge here, as prior knowledge.

Interlinking Clues

So, if you already know the answer to the clue at 2 across, for example, and have filled it in on the grid, a later clue may refer you back to that answer to either make changes to it or use parts of it again.

Confused? Let's take a look at a few examples:

24's changed world (5)

In this case, there was no 24 across, and the answer to the clue at 24 down, which we can assume has already been established, was HEART. The pointer 'changed' is telling us this is an anagram. So we mix up the letters of the first answer to find the second.

Solution: EARTH

24 on the tongue of an animal (4)

From the same puzzle, this further clue also referred us back to the answer at 24 down. This time it's a sounds familiar type clue (the pointer is 'on the tongue'), and the animal we are looking for sounds just the same as our first answer although the spelling is different.

Solution: HART

Queen replaced 51 and 6 in 16, creating King (6)

Well, with such a mixture of numbers and royal references, it's hard to know where to start. First of all, let's look at that word 'replaced' which tells us clearly that we are to do a little letter maths here and replace one or more letters with others. Now, think back to the abbreviations list in Chapter 11. The Queen could be an

R or ER, and from the Roman numerals list we know that 51 translates as LI and 6 as VI, but what about 16? There is no obvious way of converting 16 into letters, so maybe this is a red herring and something else is required? In fact, 16 here refers to clue 16 in the same puzzle, the answer to which was OBLIVION.

Now we have something to go on. Take that word OBLIVION and start replacing some of the letters as suggested. The Queen's initials ER replace both LI and VI. Now we have our king – Oberon, king of the fairies – another Shakespeare reference needing a little literary knowledge. So, all in all, this one is quite a baffling and specialised clue to tackle.

Solution: OBERON

Hold back the remaining 23 (8)

There can be no reasons for a number like 23 to appear in a clue other than as a reference to another in the same puzzle. After all, it has no usable Roman numeral equivalent and there are no sports teams with 23 players! Here we need the answer to clue 23, which was CLOUDBURST. So we know we are on a wet weather theme, and it's not hard to get to 'rain'. Another word for 'the remaining' is 'rest'. Together they make a word meaning 'hold back.'

Solution: RESTRAIN

Want to own one, one under seven, so got smarter (8)

If 'want' becomes 'need', and that word then owns or includes 'a' as in 'one', then all we need to get to grips with is the reference to 'one under seven' which also has to be 'owned' or dropped inside. It can't be the rather obvious six, as this just doesn't fit. So, again we need to think laterally. The only other 'seven' on offer is clue number seven in the same puzzle. There may of course, as in any example of this clue type, be both a 7 across and a 7 down to choose from, but in the puzzle this clue came from there was just one possibility, the answer to which was 'eleven'. Now, one under seven becomes 'ten' and all the elements can fit together to arrive at the solution.

Solution: NEATENED'

14 A Box of Tricks

The more puzzles you work on, the more you will learn to recognise some of the regular tricks employed to try to throw you off the scent and mislead you into blind alleys and wrong assumptions.

CLEVER TWISTS TO REMEMBER

Some tricks and twists crop up time and again, so they are worth learning off by heart, or at least keeping the following list close at hand to help you spot them. It would be impossible to provide a definitive list, but here, arranged in alphabetical order, are some of the more common trick words I have encountered (and what they might *really* mean). I hope they help!

The Usual Suspects

Articles: a, an or the

Base: e, as in mathematics

Bridge: often refers not to a structure but to the game and its four players – N, S, E or W

Butter: not a dairy product, but one who butts – usually a ram or goat

Circle: the letter O (circles: OO)

Debts: IOUs, a very useful and common word ending

Diamonds: ice

Eight: not a Roman numeral, but a rowing eight, commonly used in clues that mention crew or oars

Flower: not usually a bloom, but a river

Left: can be L, but often means port, as on board a ship

Low: not always a positional reference, but an animal sound – usually moo

Nothing: either nil or the letter O

On board: referring to a ship, so SS may be somewhere in the answer

One: can be ace, the letter I, or more likely a or an

Op: a common abbreviation for work

Party: do

Piano: not the instrument, but the musical term p, meaning soft or quiet

Popular: in

Quarters: another way of referring to the four compass points, N, S, E and W.

Ring: not jewellery or phone calls, but the letter O

Say: can lead you towards a sound-alike clue, but often means e.g., as in for example

See: often crops up meaning a bishop's diocese rather than anything eyesight connected

Setter: I or me, as in the crossword's setter or compiler

Sex appeal: IT

Space: not usually rockets and stars, but the simple word em, a printing term

Spies: CIA

Story: could be a tale or saga, but is often a lie

Turn: can be a U, but often translates as go, as in taking a turn when playing a game

Variable: usually means the letter x, y or z, as in algebra

Volunteers: TA, as in Territorial Army

Weekend: can be either the abbreviation WE, or K (the end of the word 'week')

Working: on, as in an electrical appliance or light being switched on

Writer: could be a pen, but usually refers to me or I, as in the crossword's compiler

15 Now It's Your Turn

Now it's your turn to have another go at solving a few clues, this time based on what we have learned in Chapters 11 to 14. The following ten clues are a mixture of abbreviations, foreign words, general knowledge and our commonly used box of tricks, although some of the other cryptic elements we have looked at in earlier chapters may creep in too!

In each case, look out for the pointer (if any) to determine which type (or types) of clue it is, and then try to solve it. Clues are arranged in approximate order of difficulty, easiest first. If you get stuck a brief explanation appears alongside each solution.

MORE CLUES FOR PRACTICE

Clue 1: Setter's beginning to punish little pest (3)

Clue 2: Witch overcomes soldiers with this dish (6)

Clue 3: Harris flipped popular old coin (6)

Clue 4: Parisian is in Cork in order to fill shelves again (7)

Clue 5: False story, say, about Belgian city (5)

Clue 6: In church, I talk gibberish, similar to a Persian perhaps? (3-4)

Clue 7: Gore and Eisenhower are similar (5)

Clue 8: Quiet fellow cracks a cryptic clue after training (8)

Clue 9: Mysterious tomb with diamonds lacking finish (7)

Clue 10: Warmest lettuce that is available on street (7)

The Solutions

Clue 1: IMP

The setter here is I (the compiler of the puzzle) from our box of tricks list, with 'I am' shortened down to I'm (minus the apostrophe, of course). The beginning that's mentioned is the pointer to using the first letter only of the word 'punish'. Put both elements together to find the pest required.

Clue 2: HAGGIS

Soldiers, as you may remember from the abbreviations listed in Chapter 11, may be GIs. And another name for a witch is a hag. She 'overcomes' them simply by going first. Easy!

Clue 3: FLORIN

There are two elements of general knowledge at play here – famous names and coinage. Who can you think of with the surname Harris? The answer here is the entertainer Rolf Harris, and the pointer 'flipped' tells us to read his name backwards, adding 'in' (meaning popular) from our box of tricks list, to find the name of a discontinued British coin.

Clue 4: RESTOCK

'In order' is a pointer, telling us to change the order of the letters and make an anagram of 'cork'. The other pointer 'Parisian' hints at something French. We have to use the French word for 'is' (which is 'est') and put it inside the anagram letters to find the solution.

111

Clue 5: LIEGE

From the box of tricks list, a story, and especially a false one, is a lie. Those three letters now need to go 'about' something that means 'say' – not as in 'speak', but as in 'for example', or the abbreviation e.g. Some general knowledge is needed too, in order to identify the city name required.

Clue 6: CAT-LIKE

Here the pointer 'gibberish' is leading us towards something garbled or mixed-up, i.e. an anagram of 'I talk', but the anagram letters have to appear 'in church'. One of the recognised abbreviations for the church is C.E., standing for Church of England. Put those two letters around the outsides, and we find why the answer may be similar to a Persian, which is of course a breed of cat.

Clue 7: ALIKE

This is a very easy and straightforward clue if you know your American politicians. It's just their two first names side by side, with the answer meaning 'similar'. But if you are too young to remember them or have never heard of them, things get a bit trickier!

Clue 8: PEACEFUL

Here we have the unusual and pertinent pointer word, 'cryptic', which points us towards an anagram of 'a clue', along with two abbreviations – f for fellow, who cracks the anagram by appearing inside it, and PE for physical exercise (or training) which the clue tells us must come at the start. The answer means 'quiet'.

Clue 9: CRYPTIC

And in the same vein...the tomb is of course a crypt, and from our box of tricks we use the word 'ice' to mean diamonds – although here the final letter is missing because the diamonds are unfinished.

Clue 10: COSIEST

Do you know your varieties of lettuce? The one we need here is a 'cos', and it is followed by two abbreviations – i.e., from the Latin meaning 'that is', and the more well-known 'st' for street. And the warmest is, of course, the cosiest.

16 Now It's Your Turn – Advanced

When you get stuck on a particular clue in a newspaper puzzle (which all of us do from time to time), it may mean waiting an anxious day or two until you have access to the published solutions. But, even then, there will be no explanation given – just the answer. Sometimes there is nothing else for it but to put your thinking cap on and work out where that answer came from for yourself. If that happens to you, go back over some of the examples and explanations in this book. No matter how difficult a clue you may encounter, everything you need to know to crack it is here!

In this final list of clues, I have saved some of the most devious examples until last. Here we have clues that use multiple combinations of clue types and techniques, or that require very specific knowledge, or involve some tricky spelling or unusual vocabulary. Many of them are adapted from clues that originated in some of the hardest daily or Sunday newspaper crosswords. These clues may require more thought, more effort and more time to crack.

And now for the bad news... Although the solutions are listed later, I am not going to offer any explanations this time. Take a sneaky peek at the answers if you must, but working out how they are arrived at and fully understanding them is going to be up to you.

FINAL CLUES FOR PRACTICE

Clue 1: It helps solver decipher brief notice in journal (10)

Clue 2: Snow leopard's vulnerable? Collect £1000 for charity event (9, 4)

Clue 3: They can make easy cutters, pruning thorny ends (9)

Clue 4: Traders here spoil fine fabric kept jumbled inside (11)

Clue 5: French queen dances on telly regularly many times (10)

Clue 6: Lauren carrying king's child; he was starting from a desperate position (5,2,3,4)

Clue 7: Reportedly in favour after man covers top of window with piece of wood (3-2-4)

Clue 8: Director gets agitated reporting to me (4,9)

Clue 9: The pens or anything used primarily as a writer (7)

Clue 10: Cricket side at Oval smoothly added to score (6)

The Solutions

Clue 1: DICTIONARY

Clue 2: SPONSORED WALK

Clue 3: SECATEURS

Clue 4: MARKETPLACE

Clue 5: FREQUENTLY

Clue 6: BACKS TO THE WALL

Clue 7: TWO-BY-FOUR

Clue 8: OTTO PREMINGER

Clue 9: THOREAU

Clue 10: LEGATO

17 And Finally...

In this book I have tried to cover all the possible clue types you are likely to encounter, all the techniques you are likely to need, and a few of the little tricks that just might get thrown into your path, as you start to tackle the crosswords that I hope will soon become a regular and enjoyable part of your daily life.

Whether you are completely new to crosswords, are just trying to improve your knowledge and vocabulary, or are taking a step up towards ever harder puzzles, I would like to think that the tips and examples you have seen here will help to make all those future convoluted and confusing clues that you come up against much clearer, easier and satisfying to solve.

If you are just learning, take it slowly. Start with a fairly elementary puzzle book or one of the easier daily newspaper puzzles. Set yourself the challenge of completing one puzzle a day, and doing it more and more quickly each time and, only when it no longer presents you with any difficulty, move up a notch and make a start on a crossword at the next level.

There is always help available if you want to cheat, via websites and phone lines where answers are shared, or by looking at the answer pages in the back of the book. Try your best to resist them!

There really is nothing more satisfying than managing to crack a crossword all by yourself, no matter how long it takes. And, if you sometimes feel that you have to give up, make sure you get hold of a copy of the solution when it is published, so you can find out the answer to the clue that was stumping you. Then try to analyse it. Unless it has been very badly constructed, every word in a clue is there for a reason. Look for the pointers, spot the tricks, and break the clue and the answer down into their component parts, so you can make sense of how they were put together, and why. When you see the solution in print, hopefully all will become clear and you will wonder why you couldn't solve it in the first place.

Remember what I said in the introduction to this book. A daily dose of crossword action can help to relax you, keep your brain cells working, make your mind quicker and sharper, improve your spelling and your memory, and extend your vocabulary. It sounds like some kind of wonder drug for holding back the years!

But crosswords are much more than just therapy for a tired or ageing brain. They can so easily become a hobby, a habit, a necessity, or even an obsession. However hooked you get, try to remember that they are supposed to be fun too.

Happy puzzling!